THE ANNUAL
OUTING
and Other Excursions

By The Same Author

Victorian Entertainment
Have You Forgotten Yet?:
Between the Two World Wars
A Print Buyer's Handbook

Books for young readers

The Very Hot Water Bottle
Hide The Slipper
Winner On Points
Return Ticket
Nothing Up My Sleeve
Mile-A-Minute Ernie
Edwardian England
(Then and There Series)
Printing
A Hundred Years of Medical Care
(Then and There Series)
As They Saw Her: Florence Nightingale

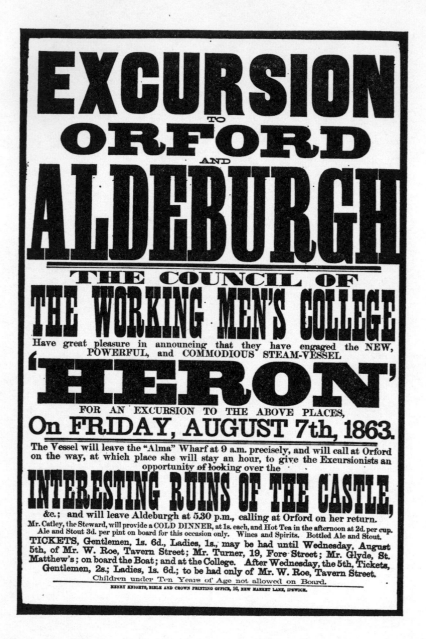

EXCURSION
TO
ORFORD
AND
ALDEBURGH

THE COUNCIL OF
THE WORKING MEN'S COLLEGE

Have great pleasure in announcing that they have engaged the NEW, POWERFUL, and COMMODIOUS STEAM-VESSEL

'HERON'

FOR AN EXCURSION TO THE ABOVE PLACES,

On FRIDAY, AUGUST 7th, 1863.

The Vessel will leave the "Alma" Wharf at 9 a.m. precisely, and will call at Orford on the way, at which place she will stay an hour, to give the Excursionists an opportunity of looking over the

INTERESTING RUINS OF THE CASTLE,

&c.; and will leave Aldeburgh at 5.30 p.m., calling at Orford on her return.

Mr. Catley, the Steward, will provide a COLD DINNER, at 1s. each, and Hot Tea in the afternoon at 2d. per cup. Ale and Stout 3d. per pint on board for this occasion only. Wines and Spirits. Bottled Ale and Stout.

TICKETS, Gentlemen, 1s. 6d., Ladies, 1s., may be had until Wednesday, August 5th, of Mr. W. Roe, Tavern Street; Mr. Turner, 19, Fore Street; Mr. Glyde, St. Matthew's; on board the Boat; and at the College. After Wednesday, the 5th, Tickets, Gentlemen, 2s.; Ladies, 1s. 6d.; to be had only of Mr. W. Roe, Tavern Street.

Children under Ten Years of Age not allowed on Board.

HENRY KNIGHTS, BIBLE AND CROWN PRINTING OFFICE, 16, NEW MARKET LANE, IPSWICH.

THE ANNUAL OUTING

and Other Excursions

Alan Delgado

London   George Allen & Unwin Ltd
Ruskin House   Museum Street

First Published in 1977

© Alan Delgado 1977

ISBN 0 04 942148 4

394.26 DEL

Printed in Great Britain
in 11/12 point Plantin type
by Butler & Tanner Ltd
Frome and London

To my sister
MARGERY

Acknowledgements

Writing a book is difficult enough, but acknowledging the help given so that it can be written, is even more difficult. So many people wrote and although their contributions may not have been used, what they sent provided helpful background material. Others directed me to useful lines of enquiry and I do thank them all sincerely. I am grateful to the archivists, curators, directors, librarians and their assistants of the libraries, record offices, societies, organisations and industrial companies listed on pages 165–7 who permitted me to research material in their possession or who sent me information which I have included in the book. The following wrote to me in vivid detail and seemed to enjoy relating their experiences as readers will discover: Mr George W. Bell, Mr T. R. Fancott, Mr William Foster, Mr E. Jarvis Garner, Mrs. A. B. Horner, Mrs E. A. Lyman, Mrs Hester Palmer, Mrs M. Pardoe, Mr C. Squires, Mr A. J. Taylor, Mrs L. Taylor, Mrs Elizabeth Tripconey, Mr H. Wilson, Mrs P. J. Willson. Mr Ronald Pearsall, author of *Victorian Popular Music* kindly supplied me with the words of 'The Excursion Train: a Tender Narrative' quoted in Chapter 1. The National Bus Company broadcast my request for information to the bus and coach companies in the group and the response was not only enthusiastic but invaluable. The Association of British Chambers of Commerce supplied me with a list of members to be approached, and the London Chamber of Commerce and Industry was also of assistance.

The extract from *Odds and Ends: A Manuscript Magazine* is included in Chapter 1 with the permission of the City of Manchester Cultural Services Department, and the verse by Harry Graham which heads Chapter 2 by permission of Messrs Edward Arnold (Publishers) Ltd.

Contents

Acknowledgements   *page* 11

Introduction   17

1   Some Early Excursions   23

2   Attitudes, Safety and Sundays   42

3   The Firm's Annual Outing 1836–1914   58

4   'To Some Poor Child A Happy Day'   77

5   Nearly all at Sea   90

6   Sunday School 'Trips' and Other Pleasures   106

7   Exhibitions and Other Events   121

8   By Charabanc Between the Wars   139

9   Exit the Day Outing, Enter the Package Holiday   154

Sources   165

Index   169

Illustrations

PLATES
(*between pages* 80 *and* 81)

1 The G. Delgado staff outing to Margate, c. 1898
'To Brighton and Back for 3s 6d.' After the painting by
Charles Rossiter. *Birmingham Museum and Art Gallery*

2 'The Excursion Train Galop.' A nineteenth-century music
cover. *The British Library*
'The Beach Hotel.' Trippers on the sands, c. 1850

3 Booking for an excursion train, 1872. *'Illustrated London
News'*
Waiting for the excursion train, 1880. *'Illustrated London
News'*

4 Trent Bridge excursion train disaster, 1869 by an artist
at the scene of the accident. *'Illustrated Midland News'*
The beach at Hastings, 1857. *'Illustrated Times'*

5 A day out in 1908 for the clerks at Cadbury's. *Cadbury
Collection, Birmingham Library*

6 'Say, Mister, is this the Godley train?' A nineteenth-
century cartoon against Sunday excursions. *Public
Record Office*

7 A day in the country for London's children, 1872.
Prayers with the provisions.

8 'Prisoners in Mean Street.' *The Shaftesbury Society*
Two 'prisoners' released. *The Shaftesbury Society*

9 Employees of Laurence, Scott on a nineteenth-century
river outing with musical accompaniment. *Laurence, Scott
& Electromotors Ltd*
Bentalls' staff at Sunbury Lock in 1910. *Bentalls*

10 The Independent Order of Good Templars Juvenile
Spring Blossom outing at Whitley Bay in 1898. *Central
Library, Newcastle*

11 Staff outing to Sir George Chubb's home in Chislehurst,
Kent, c. 1906. *Chubb & Son's Lock & Safe Co. Ltd*
Chelmsford Co-op staff outing, c. 1913. *National Travel
(South East) Ltd*

12 The leather factory employees at Charles Letts off to Southend for the day in 1912. *Charles Letts & Co. Ltd* Pilkington's bevelling department set off for a day at Blackpool in the 1920s. *Pilkington Bros Ltd*

13 To the 1924 British Empire Exhibition at Wembley: Boots of Nottingham by train. *The Boots Co Ltd* Heelas of Reading by charabanc. *The John Lewis Partnership*

14 Bedminster Ebenezer Sisterhood outing, 27 June 1922. *Bristol Omnibus Co. Ltd* Children's outing from Scunthorpe, 1925. *East Midland Motor Services Ltd*

15 First Kodak staff outing, Selsey, 3 July 1927. *Kodak Ltd*

16 Hever Castle, June 1937. Most of the Times Publishing Company staff who attended. *'The Times'*

ILLUSTRATIONS IN THE TEXT

Excursion to Orford and Aldeburgh, 1863. *Suffolk Record Office, Ipswich* frontispiece

Arrangements for G. Delgado outing to Hastings, 1894. *page* 20

Excursion to Knowsley, 1856. *District Central Library, Preston, Lancashire* 26

Cheap Trip to Llangollen, 1852. *Salop County Council* 56

Grand Pic-nic Day at Ashby-de-la-Zouch, 1850. *Thomas Cook & Son Ltd* 63

The Public Dejeuner on the occasion of the opening of Brierdean Bridge, 1840*. *His Grace the Duke of Northumberland*, K.G., T.D., D.C.L. 92

The Great Exhibition, 1851. 'To The Working Classes of Beverley.' *Humberside Record Office* 125

One Way of Writing 'Wembley'. A pictorial comment on the British Empire Exhibition, 1924. *Unilever Ltd* 129

* This document is deposited at the County Record Office, Northumberland County Council.

Introduction

This book was inspired—if that is the right word—by a photograph of my father with his workpeople on an outing to Margate at the end of the last century. The photograph, facing page 80, shows some sixty employees and their employer, all dressed in their best, and was taken outside the restaurant of the Metropole Hotel. The day's menu—described in general terms—is displayed outside. Just the words, soup, fish, entrees, joints—everything in the plural, thereby indicating abundance—but the lower half of the menu is partly obscured by an employee's bowler hat. Adjacent to the restaurant is the public bar of the hotel and the familiar red 'hand' trade mark advertising Allsopp's Burton Ale.

The photograph is an interesting fabric of social history. The men wear stiff white collars and waistcoats. The ladies, for the most part, are dressed in white with hardly a toe visible under their long skirts. Most of the headgear consists of straw hats or 'boaters'. Even my father wears one, and he can be seen in the second row from the front, eight from the right, face up towards the camera. He has a stiff, upright collar with tie, and there is a flower in the lapel of his jacket. In fact, quite a number of men and women have a buttonhole. In the group are eight bowler hats, a single homburg, five 'boaters' and a couple of uncovered male heads, but no lady's head is uncovered. A seafaring type standing on the extreme left with his fingers in the proximity of his waistcoat pocket may well have been an employee, but he could be a stranger who stopped to see what was going on.

The occasion was the annual excursion of the employees of G. Delgado who originally had premises at 2 Tower Royal, Cannon Street before moving to 17 and 18 Paradise Street, Finsbury, E.C. in 1896. He was a manufacturer of greeting cards, calendars and stationery. When the firm flourished and became a limited company it was described more grandly as 'Fine Art Publishers'. When my father moved from his original premises at Tower Royal to Paradise Street, the Notice of Removal which he sent to his business associates appropriately stated he was the manufacturer of the 'Fin de Siècle' series of Menus, Xmas Cards, Ball

B

Programmes, Birthday Cards, and all Fancy Stationery. Special mention was made on the notice that 'this Card is made throughout at my works'.

On 13 July 1893 a facetious but revealing account headed 'A Pleasant Annual Excursion' was printed in *The British & Colonial Printer and Stationer:*

'It was one of those perfect summer days that will cause the present year to be long remembered that Mr. Delgado held the annual holiday of his staff, which is occupied in the ateliers of Tower Royal in the production of those dainty English cards which have made a name for their producers . . . The excursion left the precincts of Tower Royal at the hour of nine a.m. and wended their way through the thoroughfares of the City enroute for the pretty village of Broxbourne. It could be easily seen that pleasure was 'on the cards' . . . laughter and merriment were the order of the day, while the exhilarating effect of the drive through the morning air was still further enhanced by the selection of popular airs, performed by the band of string and wind instruments retained for the occasion. After a pleasant drive of about three hours, and one or two halts for refreshments, the Crown Hotel at Broxbourne was reached, and it is worth noting that, although the party had breaks down the whole way, there had been no break down during the journey. It was a relief in one sense to disembark and look around on the pretty scene with the old Crown Hotel in the foreground. About fifty-five persons participated in this relief, and then, after adjourning to the interior of the hotel to deposit such wraps and impedimenta as they had brought with them, they sallied out into the charming grounds of the hotel to stroll along the shady walks and alleys, admire the rose garden, wander by the banks of the river Lea, flowing past the back of the hotel, and, sheltered by the avenue of limes, or resting in the bowers of weeping ash, to indulge in bucolic reveries not unmixed with feelings of hunger . . .'

Dinner was at 1.30 and, 'the well selected menu having at length come to its conclusion and tongues loosened thereby', there were speeches. The afternoon was spent on the cricket field, tennis courts, or indulging in archery, croquet and other outdoor activities. At five o'clock 'a general move was made for tea, after which there was musical entertainment carried out by the Tower Royal Artistes. The Misses West and Wright made a sensation in their vocal duet 'Very Improper Indeed' . . . The pianoforte performances were in the able hands—and nimble fingers—of Miss Purusinowski and Miss Burrow . . .'

and so on in similar vein. At about 8.30 'The party bidding adieu to this pretty spot, started on their drive home, perfectly convinced that it would have indeed been difficult to have selected a better place where they might spend a happy day.'

It was customary for my father to print a programme of events for each outing, giving instructions as to times and places of departure and return, particulars of the entertainment provided and the menu that would be set before his guests. The programmes were highly decorative. Sometimes they were cut into shapes and patterns and appropriately embellished, all of which demonstrated the skills necessary for the trade. The Royal Oak at Hastings was visited in 1894, the Alexandra Hotel, Sandgate in 1897, The Metropole Hotel, Margate in 1899, The Brunswick Hotel, Clacton in 1900, while at Brighton in 1901 luncheon was served in the Masonic Room at the Pavilion, and it was recorded that the caterer was Mutton of the King's Road. In 1902 the Plough Inn, Elstree received them.

After contemplating the material available to me that concerned the annual outings organised by my father, and recollecting the company outings (not in my father's firm) in which I had participated during the course of my working life (mainly on the river to Marlow), I considered that the subject of annual outings and excursions generally might be a rewarding piece of social history. I was further encouraged by J. A. R. Pimlott's inference in his classic book *The Englishman's Holiday* that a history of railway and other excursions could be an excellent subject for a book.

From the description of the Broxbourne outing of my father's firm which has been quoted in part, it was clear that such an event was referred to as a 'holiday', and that from the programmes in my possession it was equally clear that such outings took place on a Saturday so that only half a day's production was lost. It was not only firms that had outings. Charities sent children to the sea and countryside; the Sunday School outing was a feature of village life. There were different methods of transport, from the horse-drawn waggon to the train and charabanc (and combination of both), outings and excursions by boat—all would have to be considered. The difficulty was to unearth the information. There are descriptions of outings in literature, but not to any great extent.

Having begun, the co-operation of the County Records Offices throughout the country was invaluable. Even more encouraging were the letters I received from the public in response to one I

ᴖᴕᴖ ARRANGEMENTS. ᴖᴕᴖ

Saturday, June 16th. 1894.

9.15.	Everyone to be at Cannon Street Station, City—South Eastern Railway.
9.30.	Train leaves for Hastings—all to take their seats strictly in the order agreed upon.
11.34.	Train due at Hastings.
1.30.	Dinner at Royal Oak Hotel.
5.30.	Tea at Royal Oak Hotel.
7.30.	Everyone to be at Hastings Station—South Eastern Railway.
7.55.	Train leaves Hastings for London—Seats to be taken in same order as going.
10.36.	Arrive at Cannon Street.

In the event of wet weather, accommodation has been secured at the Royal Oak Hotel, and a piano provided.

It is expected of everyone to be strictly punctual to above-mentioned times.

wrote to newspapers seeking recollections in that sphere. There is no doubt that a strong nostalgic chord was struck by the subject. Even in what some people prefer to call the 'bad old days' there appears to have been at least one 'good' old day—the day of the annual outing. The response was most gratifying; however poor or miserable life was, this one day by the sea or in the meadows of the countryside was something remembered with pleasure.

Disappointingly there was little response from individual firms. Large companies employing an archivist or a member of the staff whose job it was to look after records were able to supply information about firms' outings that took place before the firms concerned became part of a larger unit. I am sure that tucked away in dust-laden cupboards and files there are photographs and descriptions of outings of days gone by, but finding time to look out the material, dust it down and sort it out cannot easily be spared. It was clear, too, that one outing within a given period is very like another. What makes a particular outing interesting is a personal recollection or a description that reveals an attitude or sketches an incident typical of an era.

After the Second World War the outing, as I have pointed out in the final chapter, ceased to exist in its original form; nor was the

Roast Beef.

Roast Mutton.

Boiled Mutton, Caper Sauce.

Roast Chicken and Ham.
Peas, Potatoes, &c.

Hot Royal Oak Pudding.

Gooseberry and Rhubarb Tart.

Stewed Fruit and Blanc Mange.

Cheese—Salad.

FOURTH ANNUAL EXCURSION,
G. DELGADO,
2, TOWER ROYAL, CANNON STREET,
LONDON, E.C.

need the same. The advent of faster and more sophisticated methods of travel, the changes in social attitudes and the coming of the affluent society determined that.

I had decided to concentrate on the 'day' outing and the 'day' excursion within Britain although exceptions are made. For a day outing you only have to take yourself away. If you spend a night or longer away you not only take yourself, but also luggage and other encumbrances as well. Every moment of a day outing was precious and had to be lived to the fullest especially if you were young. Going away for more than a day created quite a different situation.

The *Concise Oxford Dictionary* describes 'outing' as 'pleasure trip, holiday away from home'. It was at one time just that—a holiday away from home—even though it may have lasted no longer than a single day.

The period covered is nineteenth century up to the Second World War.

I

Some Early Excursions

'Railways . . . have opened our Island to the Pleasure Tourist; and the work of civilisation which they are thus accomplishing is not amongst the least remarkable of their consequences.'
From the Introduction to *Knight's Excursion Companion*, 1851

Before the railways straddled Britain an excursion to Brighton from London in the 1820s would be accomplished in a day by barouche. 'Quitting Islington after breakfast,' wrote a contemporary, 'we set off . . . all right merrily disposed for our withdrawment into the country . . . Passing over Blackfriar's Bridge, we soon reach Kennington. This village has been enlarged, and undergone many improvements.'

In the 1840s there were excursions by rail on the Eastern Counties, South Eastern, Brighton and South Coast, South Western and London and North Western Railways. Starting from London, the tourist was advised to catch an early train. Although horse carriages were available at the destination there was no substitute for a good walk.

In the middle of the nineteenth century there was a spate of books written to guide the new public of excursionists on their travels, pointing out the places to see, how to get there, where to eat and rest. Walton and Weybridge could be enjoyed at all times, but the best months for an excursion were the end of July or during August, when the purple heather was in full bloom. 'A ride of three quarters of an hour takes the smoke-laden inhabitant of the metropolis to a scene luxuriantly mantled with this lovely flower.' If the tourist was 'indisposed' for an excursion involving an eight-mile walk, or his 'gentle' companion felt such a walk would be 'over toilsome', it was suggested that the excursion could be divided into two parts, St George's Hill being one; Walton the other.

Routes were well sign-posted but there might be occasions when the tourist had doubts as to whether or not he was on the right road. In one instance doubt could be set at rest if he was 'saluted by a ferocious howl of a singularly ugly brute of a dog chained to a kennel at the inside of a hedge'. Having experienced this challenge, the tourist would know that he was walking in the right direction.

Every station on the Dover Railway proclaimed by poster that it was the 'pleasure line' offering tempting curiosities in abbeys, castles, mansions, parks, but it was only on the South Western Railway out of London that the tourist saw the embankments fringed with heather.

Shepperton was for anglers who chalked on the inside of public house doors the details of the fish caught, its weight and the name of the successful angler. A trout a day was considered good sport; a couple of trout was an exceptional catch.

Guildford was considered a perfect spot for a day's excursion; Winchester, with its historical associations, must also be visited. An excursion to Croydon took only four hours there and back, where the tourist 'may profitably and pleasureably walk through shaded lanes to Beddington'. Visitors to Hever were advised to alight at Edenbridge Station and hire a carriage to take them on.

A day's excursion to Cobham meant a start from Hungerford Market, London Bridge Stations or the Blackwall Railway Station in Fenchurch Street. The fare was 1s 6d and there was a choice of at least twenty-four trains throughout the day. A visit to Cobham Church was recommended for brass rubbings. Heel balls purchased at most shoeshops cost a penny for two. Cobham Hall exhibited paintings by Titian, Rubens, Holbein, Kneller and Vandyke, but one picture 'Death of Regulus' by Salvator Rosa could not be looked at 'without shuddering'. The visitor was told to conquer his disgust 'and become chilled into indifference at the horrors of the scene' before examining 'the merits of its rude vigour'.

A drawback to visiting such places as Cobham Hall was the fee to offer the housekeeper. 'It is difficult to estimate what is due to this fine lady in amber satin, with lace ruffles and tippets—gold watch and seals at her side instead of keys.' The tourist did not like to appear mean by offering as little as half-a-crown, but at Cobham Hall the fee was fixed at a shilling which saved embarrassment, and it was lamented that this example was not followed elsewhere.

'EXCURSION TO ENGLAND' announced an advertisement in the *Scotsman* of 18 August 1849, when a special train left North Bridge Station, Edinburgh at seven o'clock in the morning on 22nd of that month. The trip to England, it was announced, had been made with perfect confidence 'on account of the complete nature of the travelling arrangements, and because the district or country through which the Party will pass is famed for its varied and picturesque scenery'. On buying a ticket, each passenger was given a card with information 'of all that is to be seen in Newcastle'. The fare from Edinburgh to Newcastle and back was 15s first class; 12s second class; 9s third class.

A Select Committee on Railways in 1840 observed that railways were built 'to convey the labourer cheaply and rapidly to that spot where his labour might be most highly remunerated'. Also, the Committee added, 'the health and enjoyment of the mechanics, artisans, and poor inhabitants of the large towns would be promoted, by the facility with which they would be enabled to remove themselves and their families into healthier districts and less crowded habitations'.

Basically the railways were for the benefit of industry; the best method of moving coal from the pithead to the factories and to the areas from which it could be collected for domestic use. Human beings could be conveyed by train because it was obviously beneficial to their health if they lived away from the overcrowded towns in which industry was situated, but it was important that the railways could convey them quickly from the countryside back into the towns to work.

To-day, when over fifty per cent of manual workers have between three and four weeks annual paid holiday, it is worth remembering that the Factory Act of 1833 'entitled' certain workers to eight half-days each year as well as Christmas Day and Good Friday, but the word 'entitled' was used by unscrupulous employers as an excuse not to comply with the Act. Not until 1871 and the Bank Holiday Act and subsequent legislation were six Bank Holidays allowed in England, and five in Scotland.

The demand for cheap travel, the desire to see new places and fill the lungs with pure air was overwhelming. In 1850, Charles Knight acknowledged that 'the transit to the most distant and once most inaccessible places is rapid and cheap beyond all comparisons. Not only is the Metropolis brought into the most intimate connexion with the Provinces, but every great industrial district has its own Capital, from which centre railway-lines radiate to the

---

EXCURSION TO KNOWSLEY, the seat of the Right Hon. Earl of Derby.—The Working Men's Committee for promoting the establishment of a Free Library and Museum in Preston have the honour to announce that by the kind permission of the Right Hon. the Earl of Derby, arrangements have been made for an

EXCURSION TO KNOWSLEY AND BACK,
On Tuesday, July 15, 1856.

The train will leave Preston station at half-past nine o'clock in the morning, and return from Huyton, 1½ miles from Knowsley, at six o'clock in the evening.

Fares:—First-class, 5s.; inclosed carriages, 2s. 6d.

Tickets may be had at the following places, until seven o'clock on Monday evening, July 14, viz.:—At the *Guardian*, *Chronicle*, and *Pilot* Offices; at Worthington and Co.'s, printers, Town-hall Corner; and at the station, on the morning of the excursion. An early application for tickets is requested.

The committee have not found it practicable to make arrangements for providing the excursionists with refreshments, parties will therefore have to provide their own.

Mr. Norwood's celebrated band is engaged for the occasion.

Knowsley Hall, the seat of Lord Derby, one of the finest mansions in Lancashire, contains a valuable collection of paintings by the old masters. The park is of considerable extent. The pleasure-grounds, the lake, the beautiful boathouse, the gardens, greenhouses, and collections of exotic plants, are highly interesting. Lord Derby has generously consented to allow admission to the hall.

For the Working Men's Committee,
HENRY BRADLEY, Chairman.
THOMAS EDELSTON, Secretary.

---

remotest extremities . . .' He pointed out that the railways were no longer based entirely on commercial considerations but that 'they take us amongst mountains and lakes, the margins of the broad sea, and the banks of the smiling rivers . . .'

The excursion train was of cultural benefit. As the *Illustrated London News* pointed out in 1843, 'it is most creditable to the improved intelligence of the lower orders that they rush in thousands to the British Museum or the National Gallery' and similar places. The same journal some seven years later revealed the political significance of easy and cheap travel exemplified by the respect paid by a party of French excursionists on a visit to the Duke of Wellington. Had they never seen England, the journal pointed out, they would have remained contemptuous of the Duke, but their hearts as well as their eyes were opened and they learnt to respect a country so long considered a natural foe.

'The Excursion Train is one of our best public instructors. It is also one of the cheapest. At a rate for second and third-class passengers, varying from twenty miles to twenty-five miles for a shilling, or from little above a halfpenny to less than a farthing a mile, hundreds of thousands of travellers from London, during 1850, have been carried into the heart of our most beautiful inland scenery—to our Watering-places—to our Ports—to our Universities—to our great Seats of Manufacturers and Commerce. Upon the same principle, Excursion Trains from the Provinces have duly brought visitors to London. Nor is this all. From all the great manufacturing and commercial towns, Excursion Trains are constantly bearing the active and intelligent artisans, with their families, to some interesting locality, for a happy and national holiday. The amount of pleasure and information thus derived, and of prejudice thus removed, cannot be estimated at too high a rate.'

So wrote Charles Knight, the nineteenth-century author, publisher of encyclopedias and guide books. He sensed the burst for freedom by people compelled to live in towns created by the Industrial Revolution. The increased mobility made possible by the railways in the mid-nineteenth century revealed to millions aspects of their country about which they knew little or nothing, and made them receptive to the popular press in the guise of the *Daily Mail*, 'the penny newspaper that sold for a halfpenny' which appeared first in 1896.

An early excursion was run in 1830 by the Liverpool and Manchester Railway Company soon after the line opened, from Manchester (and presumably Liverpool) to Newton Bridge, where a large hotel had been built for the entertainment of excursionists. A correspondent, writing in 1890, recollects riding on horseback with his brother from Broom Hill, Pendlebury, on Saturday afternoons to see the trains on the way to Manchester. The hotel eventually became a printing works.

In *The Times* of 29 May 1838 the London and Southampton Railway advertised extra trains to the Epsom Races:

> 'The public are informed that, with a view to accommodate the visiters [sic] to Epsom Races, EXTRA TRAINS will RUN on Tuesday, Wednesday, Thursday and Friday from Vauxhall to that point of the railway to the south of Kingston which is nearest Epsom.'

This entailed hiring a carriage or undertaking a considerable walk from the train and back after what might or might not have been a profitable day. The fares were 2s 6d first class; 1s 6d second class.

In August 1849 A FEMALES' CHEAP TRIP was announced from Preston to Fleetwood, starting from Maudland Station at 8.30 a.m. and returning to Preston at 7 p.m. Females' tickets and those for schools and children under twelve years of age cost 9d return. Men, it appears, could be included but they had to pay 1s 6d return.

> 'The arrangements will afford an opportunity to a vast number of females who were anxious to purchase tickets for the last trip but being a charity one could not be allowed. Employees, also, who do not arrange for trips on their own account, may avail themselves of this opportunity of sending down any of the sick or other hands whom they may be desirous of treating. A steamer will ply through the day to take persons round the Light-house at 2d each. Arrangements can also be made for Bathing in the Victoria Baths at a low charge; and (weather permitting) for outdoor amusements.'

Those going were told to be at the station ten minutes before departure and to take their seats without delay. Friends, it was pointed out, would find them easier in a carriage than in a crowd. Tickets must be ready to show. A lost ticket meant having to pay a return fare, so it was advisable to keep it in a safe place. 'Above all things show an accommodating disposition, and a wish to oblige; this will materially assist in making the excursion pleasant.' Passengers were urged not to attempt to leave their seats till the train was fully stopped at Fleetwood. Finally, do not bathe too near the promenade.

Sea bathing for the working classes in Lancashire on Sundays was organised by the Lancashire & Yorkshire Railway c. 1850. Parties availing themselves of the trains 'will be entitled to BATHE AND REFRESH THEMSELVES in ample time to attend a place of Worship'. In 1845 an omnibus called 'The Safety' ran trips from Colne and Burnley to Simpson's Hotel, Blackpool, for the purpose of sea bathing.

In 1853 the first rail excursion to Deeside was advertised by the Deeside Railway. Announced as a 'Pleasure Trip to Upper Banchory' it was under the auspices of the Aberdeen Temperance Society. Those who were entitled to buy tickets must be members of the Society 'and others friendly to its objects'. Fares from Aberdeen to Banchory and back were 1s third class; 1s 6d first class.

A day in the country or by the sea was beneficial to health as guide books of the period stressed: 'After a Sunday at the coast, each individual seems more eager than another to resume the battle of business . . . There is a freshness in every face, a buoyancy in every step . . . Wan faces become tinged with a browness borrowed from the sun, and unkempt locks suggest a familiar acquaintance with the misty mountain winds . . .'

In 1850 a Dr Bremmer purchased a house in the village of Dovercourt 'whither, so often as his professional avocations permitted, he was accustomed to repair for the relaxation of the mind, and the improvement of his bodily health'. A hearty type, the doctor went with friends on an outing from Dovercourt to Walton and The Sokens. He positively glowed with rude health and impressed upon those with him 'the salutary effects to be derived from rising with the lark and enjoying the new-born day with all its invigorating influences'. It was quite usual for the doctor 'to have returned from a plunge in the sea before the rest of the party had risen from their beds'.

Food and drink were of great importance to the success of an outing as they were in later years. Most people brought their own food with them, much to the dismay of local traders, but for those who could afford to pay for their meals there was pleasurable anticipation at the prospect of a good, well-served dinner. It was some recompense for an early start and an uncomfortable journey. A book on pleasure excursions, published in 1847, informed readers of worthwhile eating places in the manner of a nineteenth-century *Good Food Guide*. For example, close by Weybridge Station was The Head and Spear, 'a pretty inn, with an Italian outline' where the tourist was treated well, while at Walton Mary Copp matched anyone at stewing eels in port wine. An infallible guide to a good establishment was a clean mustard pot on the table. A mustard pot encrusted with a stale, dry mustard denoted slovenly service. Dinner at the White House, Reigate, consisting of joint, followed by exquisite fritters and cream, cost 2s 6d, all served with the luxury of a napkin, finger glass and 'tingling hot plates'. The distant whistle of the train was an unwelcome sound indicating, as it did, that it was time for the tourist to return home.

'Provisions for Treats' were advertised in 1882 by Tabbutt & Co., Melton Mowbray, consisting of Melton Mowbray Pork Pies, Veal and Ham Pies, Epicure Pies, Potted Beef, Chicken, Ham and Tongue Sausage, but the Rev. Francis Kilvert in his diaries reveals how he enjoyed more exotic fare such as grapes and claret on a mossy bank at Rosewarne, followed by dinner at eight o'clock and a most admirable conger eel. On arriving home at midnight there was a hot supper of roast fowl. A picnic at Crug in Wales, where lunch was taken in a sheltered corner, consisted of grouse, snipe, champagne and plenty of fruit and other substantial edibles. At tea there was sherry and soda water.

The *Illustrated Times* in 1857 had this to say about the shoal of Londoners who visited Hastings, not for the food but for a 'mouthful of fresh air'. The excursionists

'swarm upon the beach, wandering listelessly about with apparently no other aim than to get a mouthful of fresh air. You may see them in groups of three or four: the husband—a pale, overwrought man, dressed in black frock-coat, figured waistcoat

and bright blue tie—carried the baby; the wife, equally pale and
thin, decked out in her best, labours after with a basket of "prog".*
And then there is generally another child, one remove above the
baby, wandering aimlessly behind. She must bear the burden
until church-time is over; and the public houses will be open, a
quart of porter in the pewter will be forthcoming and the family
will dine *alfresco* on the beach.'

A music hall song entitled 'The Excursion Train', described as a
'tender narrative', was sung by E. Marshall at the Canterbury
Hall about 1860. It was written expressly for him by W. F.
Vandervell. The music, borrowed from various sources, was
arranged by Willem Vandervell. The 'story' song in rollicking
style, is worth relating as it conveys manners and modes of the
period.

The 'I' of the song invites his girl, Mary Jane, to Brighton one
Monday by train. The fare is only half-a-crown. ('Isn't it cheap ?')

> We walked to the station without any fuss
> Tho' I think Mary Jane would have liked a *Buss*,
> I forked out a sov, 'Two Thirds' did cry,
> Collared the tickets and was then shoved by,
> No change could I see and all I could hear,
> Was 'move on young man there,
> And keep the coast clear,'
> Hark there goes the Bell,
> Ah! There goes the Train,
> 'Don't stop for the change, Love,' exclaims Mary Jane,
> To her wishes of course I must bow
> Left my change and got in anyhow.

Once in the train the talk amongst the excursionists is how they
are going to spend the day—bathing, fishing, rowing, perhaps.
As the train thunders through the tunnels the boys are trying to
kiss the girls. 'That will do,' the females cry. 'You'll spoil my
things. Be quiet, pray.' But—

> When in the light,
> Ah! what a sight,
> My face is scratched, my eye is blue,
> There is no doubt I got served out,
> For something that I didn't do.

* food for a journey or excursion.

Mary Jane complains about his conduct and makes a row, but the young man rejoices to hear a voice roar, 'Tickets ready now.'

> We did alight I made all right
> And to the Beach did haste away
> Eight hours to be by the Deep Sea,
> Oh! isn't this the time of day.

Mary Jane wants to bathe, so they go to 'Fanny Huggets' and for a bob was 'scrubbed and rubbed beneath the Deep, Deep, Sea!' She looked so clean and nice afterwards that he also has a bob's worth. Then he's off to a Gents' Bathing Machine and is soon in the sea.

> Over the billows I do the Grand
> And wink my eye at the Girls on Land.

Then he hears a shout from Mary Jane. 'My Crinoline, oh, it's floating out to sea.' He rescues it, nearly drowning in the attempt. Sadly

> From the bustle we both sneaked away,
> She wouldn't be seen again that day,
> And the only word I heard her say,
> Was 'my Hoop de Doo-dem doo'
> To the nearest Tavern we did hie,
> I left her there, and said good-bye.

On his own, he returns to the beach where a Jack Tar invites him to try a sail, but

> The Sea, the Sea, the open Sea,
> Makes a precious sight too free with me.
> Oh! there's a lurch, Oh! there's a bound
> I wish they'd *heave too* and run her aground.

He appeals to the Captain who 'pays no attention to what I endure'. The Captain standing firmly on his sea legs exclaims, 'What matter? What matter? T'will do you no end of good.' On land at last, sick and ill, our hero seeks Mary Jane for consolation and finds her with a Rifleman who, she says, is a relative, but that doesn't wash. Foaming with rage he challenges the Rifleman to a fight and loses two teeth before making it up with his opponent. The rest of the time is spent in drinking hot brandies until it is time to return to London. Mary Jane, the Rifleman and our hero pack into a Third Class carriage, the last named's head 'is running round'. Horrors! He's lost the tickets!

> Although I protest in vain
> Shall have to part again
> Or they will we detain
> Send us to quod.

So he gets into a first-class carriage and has to pay fifteen bob for the privilege. On arriving back in London he loses Mary Jane, but finds her in a pub where he goes to drown his sorrows in drink. He quarrels with her, gets involved in a brawl, ruins his best suit of clothes, lets fly with a right and a left, gets one in the eye for his trouble, and is floored. The police are called,

> And being kicked in the street,
> Wound up my *Half-crown Treat*
> By Excursion Train.

In Maugham's *Liza of Lambeth** (first published in 1897) there is a description of an outing to Chingford. 'The hampers were brought out and emptied, and the bottles of beer in great profusion made many a thirsty mouth thirstier.' When the coachman shouted 'Come along, lidies an' gentlemen—if you are gentlemen, the animals is now going ter be fed.' Then they got down to it,

'pork pies, saveloys, cold potatoes, hard-boiled eggs, cold bacon, veal, ham, crabs and shrimps, cheese, butter, cold suet-puddings and treacle, gooseberry-tarts, cherry-tarts, butter, bread, more sausages, and yet again pork pies! They devoured the provisions like ravening beasts, stolidly, silently, earnestly, in large mouthfuls which they shoved down their throats unmasticated . . . They never stopped except to drink, and at each gulp they emptied their glasses; no heel-taps! And still they ate, and still they drank—but as all things must cease, they stopped at last, and a long sigh of contentment broke from their two-and-thirty throats.'

The Rev. Francis Kilvert, an inveterate excursionist, obtained considerable benefit from his journeys and described them vividly

* Heinemann

c

in his diaries. In the early 1870s, one July, Kilvert left Chippenham at 11.35 a.m. by the down mail train with a tourist ticket for Truro. He describes the scene:

'the first few miles of Cornwall looked bleak, barren and uninteresting, the most striking feature being the innumerable mine works of lead, tin and copper crowning the hills with their tall chimney shafts and ugly white dreary buildings, or nestling in a deep valley defiling and poisoning streams with the white tin washing. The country soon grew prettier, the prevailing feature of the landscape being low rounded hills like those of Radnorshire divided by very deep narrow valleys or ravines which the great timber viaducts crossed continually at a ghastly height in the air. The hill sides were clothed with a rich luxuriance of wood, chiefly oak. A man was mowing oats. Purple heather bloomed in great bunches and bushes along the railway embankments, like broom with us. A sea fog, which enveloped the hills like a mist of small rain and blotted out the distance, crept up the valleys along the streams and rose against the dark green oakwoods.'

On another occasion he travelled from Truro to Penzance by train. He was met at the station by a small wagonette with a bay and a grey. A certain amount of difficulty was experienced in stowing all the hampers on board. Driving along the beach for some way and then turning inland, the party came to an oak tree arched completely over the road. 'The driver, Edward Noy, said that no other oak arched the road between this place and London.' Land's End proved to be 'a little triangular point of rock reached by passing round the seaward side of a tall, upright shaft of cliff. I like Penzance,' he wrote. 'We drove down the old Market Chapel under repair where several coffined children have lately been found stopped into holes and corners of the roof. Probably they were unbaptized children.' He remarked that Penzance people and especially the women were said to be the handsomest in Cornwall.

On Monday, 9 August 1852, a cheap train of the Lancs and Yorks Railway Co. left Normanton Station in Yorkshire for Harrogate, Knaresborough and Ripon for Fountain's Abbey, Studley Park. The return first-class fare was 5s 6d, and 3s 6d by covered car. Children under twelve went half-price. Admission to Studley Grounds was an additional 6d. The descriptions of what was to be seen are eloquent and in the context of the period as compelling as those of to-day. It was pointed out in the announcement that Ripon was

'celebrated for its Venerable Cathedral. In the immediate vicinity is Studley Royal, with its far famed Park consisting of about 650 acres, well stocked with Deer, presenting a rich and varied aspect of graceful Hill and swelling eminence—is well wooded and beautifully interspersed with Plantations, Lawns, Statuary, and Ornamental Buildings. On the south side of the Park, in a deep Vale, through which flows the Skell rivulet, stand the Ruins of Fountains Abbey which is ranked amongst the fairest of Structures in England, and when complete spread over 12 acres, three of which are still occupied by its Magnificent Ruins.'

A fascinating account of an outing from Manchester to Rhyl sets the Victorian scene to perfection and describes attitudes much less stuffy than one might imagine. It appeared in *Odds and Ends: A Manuscript Magazine* published in 1869. 'Our Excursion to Rhyl' is by James R. Finch. Initially the author greets 'merry Whitsuntide with its festivities and merry-makings, its excursions and picnics', and points out that the party had to be 'up with the lark' to be in time for the train leaving Ordsall Lane Station at 5.45 a.m.

'We had engaged overnight the services of a good-natured policeman to knock us up at four o'clock. . . . I am afraid we caused him more trouble than he had bargained for, and he had to knock long and loudly enough to have awakened the entire neighbourhood . . . We had the streets very much to ourselves, the few persons abroad being mostly knockers-up, with their long rods, awaking the sleepy and dream-wrapt sons and daughters of labour; sundry small newspaper-vendors, already lustily crying the morning papers; a few homeless city arabs, crouching in doorways and shivering in the chill morning air; one or two in whom we could recognise the habitual early-riser, with clear shaved face and well-blacked shoes . . .

The weather was fine, so overcoats, waterproofs and umbrellas were left behind. On arriving at Ordsall Lane Station there was bustle and confusion but the party had time to look around before taking their places in the train. At one end of the station was a blind tin-whistle player who performed to a very select audience a 'choice selection of popular airs'. At last the party was warned to take their seats in the train for Rhyl and Betws-y-Coed, and after the railway officials had shouted and poked their heads through the carriage windows, the journey started.

'. . . we soon were plunging and steaming away merrily, station after station darting past in quick succession . . . The air was fragrant with the odour of the new-cut hay, and the perfume of the hawthorn. The birds were cheerily chirping their morning ditties. The cattle were lazily chewing their cud staring wonderingly at the rushing and snorting monster which swiftly sped along the iron track and all nature seemed in harmony with the joyous occasion. The morning was beautifully fine, the sun breaking through the eastern skies . . .

'Our neighbours in the next compartment had been busily engaged in thumping at the partition which separated us, almost from the time we had left Manchester, which some of our party returned with equal pertinacity.'

The train stopped at Warrington, Chester, Prestatyn, and on arrival at Rhyl the party made their way into the town for breakfast. By the time breakfast was over and they had had a good wash it was 11 a.m. Plans were made to go by train to Rhuddlan, thence by road to Bodelwyddan and round to St Asaph and then, if possible, to get as far as Cefn Rocks and Coves, and return by early train from St Asaph to Rhyl. This was achieved and the party arrived back at Rhyl at about half-past five

'and on leaving the station fell in with several young lady friends with whom we walked down the promenade. The ladies used their utmost to persuade us that donkey-riding, at a place like Rhyl, was not only permissible but fashionable . . . a few minutes afterwards we were engaged in treaty with a crowd of sun-burnt donkey-women . . . who succeeded eventually in inducing us to bestride eight of the best conducted asses in the principality . . . The saddle of one of the donkeys, on which was riding a young lady of manifold attraction, turned completely round tossing his fair burden into a pool of muddy sea-water. Fortunately the lady was not much hurt . . .'

To leave Rhyl without a sail was unthinkable, although the treacherous sands made boarding a boat difficult, and the ladies' stockings and skirts were covered with sand and sea-water.

'As the boat lay a good way out . . . the boatman had no easy task to perform in carrying eight by no means puny specimens of humanity into the boat. The ladies were taken in his arms and carried into the boat first; then the gentlemen jumped on his back, two at a time, at the imminent risk of capsizing into the sea.'

Due to the weight in the boat they were unable to get more than a few hundred yards from the shore. They arrived back at the station a few minutes before the train was due to leave for Manchester. On the station they had found a sweeping-brush head with which they disposed of the superfluous dirt from their boots and they 'were privileged also to perform the same office for the ladies, whose boots, stockings and skirts were in a most deplorable state, from the mud and sea-water'.

On the way home

'we beguiled the time with songs and hymns from the little hymn book with which we were supplied; varying the music with riddles and forfeits, in which, by reason of our dulness, we lost nearly every moveable article about us'.

The party arrived at Ordsall Lane Station

'pretty well tired but thoroughly satisfied with our day's excursion. So ended our trip to Rhyl and first visit to Wales, and we must confess that we do not remember such a thoroughly enjoyable day before . . .'

Readers of Maugham's *Liza of Lambeth* may remember that Liza's indecision as to whether or not she should go on the Bank Holiday outing to Chingford was largely overcome at the sight of a man leaving the public house carrying a horn, and 'if there was anything she adored it was to drive along to the tootling of a horn'.

It was a beautiful day and 'the coachman cracked his whip, the trumpeter tootled his horn, and with a cry and a cheer from the occupants, the brake clattered along the road'.

A start had been made early in the morning and 'as the hour grew later the streets became more filled and the traffic greater'. Once on the road to Chingford they caught up with other vehicles going in the same direction '—donkey-shays, pony-carts, trades-men's carts, dog-carts, drags, brakes, every conceivable kind of wheel-thing, all filled with people . . . they exchanged cheers and greetings as they passed, the Red Lion brake being noticeable above all for its uproariousness'.

Osbert Sitwell recalls in the second volume of autobiography, *The Scarlet Tree*,* his excitement as a child at his first charabanc excursion in about 1910 from Scarborough to Filey and back, a journey of under twenty miles which was completed in 'a breath-taking hour and a quarter'. His father, being ill, was not informed of the expedition. On the day his mother, who usually got up in time for luncheon, expressed her willingness to be ready to leave the house at half-past nine and the fact that she was ready on time made the occasion all the more important. He describes the scene:

'My aunt called for us. She and my mother wore on their heads enormous cloth caps, several layers of thick veils fell over their faces, and all three were enclosed in layer after layer of coats and mufflers. We drove to the appointed starting-place in a cab, and arrived several minutes before the charabanc was due to leave . . . I shall never forget climbing up the several steps into that very high, open conveyance, and waiting with a tremulous sense of expectancy for it to start. What made, I think, both the waiting and the starting seem yet more strange was the rudimentary character of such a vehicle. It was built as though to be drawn by horses, but it was the same height from the ground and, as one looked over the dizzy gap that hung above the almost invisible bonnet of the engine into space, one suffered the most violent feeling of disproportion, as though in a boat that ended flat with-out a prow, for one missed the glossy animal extension of the carriage . . . Now an intense excitement succeeded to this vertigo, for two men were with some difficulty winding up the

* Macmillan

dangerous machine. Soon, with a new sense of freedom and lightness, we were speeding down the steep streets, up the long hills, and out of town, along the narrow, dusty country roads of those days.'

On arrival at Filey there was relief at having reached their destination safely, but it was unwise to boast because the unknown perils of the journey back loomed ahead. 'We discussed the dust, the noise and vibration, and declared our enthusiasm for this method of travelling.'

Many books have been written about Thomas Cook, the pioneer of excursions, who was born in 1808 and began his working life as a journeyman wood-turner and temperance missionary. On 9 June 1841 he walked the fifteen miles from Market Harborough to Leicester to attend a temperance meeting at the Leicester Amphitheatre. He read of the opening of an extension of the Midland Counties Railway, and although knowing little about railways realised that they might be used to further the temperance cause.

It had been arranged to hold a large temperance meeting at a later date at Loughborough, and it occurred to Cook that if the railway could be persuaded to run a special train from Leicester to Loughborough the success of the occasion would be assured. He received permission to make the necessary arrangements if it could be done, and his efforts were successful. Therefore, on 5 July 1841, 570 passengers were conveyed from Leicester to Loughborough in a train drawn by two four-wheeled engines with fourteen open third-class passenger carriages, and one first-class carriage at the rear in which one seat was occupied by the guard. Cook was the first person to hire a special train *at his own risk*, sell railway tickets to the public and travel on the train himself to attend to the comfort of his passengers.

A year previously, in July, the Committee of the Nottingham Mechanical Institution, wishing their members to visit Leicester Exhibition, hired a special train but initially secured the names of those wanting to travel. No risk was involved, and later in the year the Midland Counties Railway advertised publicly special trains from Leicester to Nottingham and the surrounding villages.

A description of the latter occasion appeared in the *Leicester Chronicle*:

'The gallery over the esplanade at the station house was crowded with elegantly dressed females, in front of whom the band of the Duke of Rutland was stationed, and from time to time enlivened the listeners with some of its best pieces. At 11.30 alarm was felt at the non-appearance of the train. An engine with several of the railway labourers started off to meet it. Another feverish half-hour crept on, when a second engine carrying a few of the directors was despatched. At half-past twelve, however, a thin vapour, a little smoke, then a huge undulating mass was discovered at the extremity of the horizon and gave assurance that all was safe . . .'

The Leicester Journal continues the story:

'The enormous train of nearly seventy passengers passed majestically in review before the astonished spectators. It was indeed a wonderful scene. Grand! magnificent! sublime! were the terms which gave vent to the feelings as in countless succession the animated mass rushed into view. It was in truth a moving city, with banners and music and accompaniments all the material of high excitement to enhance its efficacy.'

The success of Thomas Cook's first excursion train made him realise that wood-turning was not to be his life work, but that he could serve the community best by simplifying travel for the man- and woman-in-the-street. 'O, Mr Cook,' he was told by a grateful participant of one of his mid-century excursions, 'I wish it was in my power to tell you how much we owe you for these cheap excursions. Only think, for a few shillings, I, a poor working man, have been enabled to see the glories of this fine old city—the Minster, the city walls, the old gateway, the Flower Show . . . that I could never have seen but for your special train from Nottingham to-day.' There is no doubt that Cook was genuinely concerned for the welfare and safety of his customers. 'I have often thought,' he wrote,

'that the loss of a passenger, if occasioned by any neglect or carelessness in the working of one of my trains, would deprive me of all heart to pursue this work; and I cannot but rejoice and feel thankful to the Father of mercies for the safe preservation of NEARLY A MILLION of travellers under my arrangements . . . The servants of Companies who have co-operated with me know that nothing would be more detestable to me than to see them sneaking into refreshment rooms and drinking shops . . .'

In 1844 Parliament compelled railway companies to run cheap trains daily, a cheap train meaning one in which passengers were not charged more than a penny a mile. It was not at first appreciated that the cost of running a train from A to B with a few passengers paying a high fare could be no greater if a thousand passengers were carried at a low fare. Once the profitability of cheap fares was realised, thousands of special trips and then the excursion became an industry of great benefit to the public and the railways.

Others, inspired by the trail laid by Thomas Cook, entered the excursion travel market. There was room for competition then and some of the great tour operators of to-day have their origins in the nineteenth and early twentieth centuries when travel for the masses was confined mainly to the boundaries of Britain, the main methods of transport being by train and boat.

2

Attitudes, Safety and Sundays

'I collided with some "trippers"
In my swift De Dion Bouton;
Squashed them out as flat as kippers,
Left them "aussi mort que mouton".
What a nuisance "trippers" are!
I must now repaint the car.'
Most Ruthless Rhymes by Harry Graham

The English seaside resort in the early nineteenth century had been a haven of peace and quiet for the wealthy who, if they did not possess a coach to convey them, hired one. The public coach was unpunctual and passengers had little time to eat their meals. The food was of poor quality and the cost excessive; the service was indifferent. A coach with four horses travelled at ten miles an hour, so no great distance could be covered for a short holiday. Therefore, once a resort was reached the holidaymakers were inclined to stay for some while.

The railways brought the day excursionist and transformed the peace and quiet into a babel of noise. With the people came the entertainment. Itinerant musicians, German bands, barrel organs, played non-stop. The wealthy curled up in horror and withdrew to the Continent where, it was hoped, the English Channel would form an effective barrier against the invasion of privacy. Nevertheless there was a hard core of holidaymakers who did not like foreigners or their way of life. Bernard H. Becker in his book *Holiday Haunts*, published in 1884, stated the case for them:

'There is a very large class of English folk who, not liking foreign habits or the cost of foreign travel, enjoy our magnificent seaside resorts ... so long as they are kept fairly clear of the "tripper", who brings in his train the donkeys, the brass bands, the organs, the Punch and Judy, and other nuisances ... The Nathaniel Bumppo of holidaymakers is ever moving on, driven away and away by railways and "trippers". Middle-aged people will recollect the scare produced at Brighton by the invasion of thousands who wanted their "sniff of the briny", and enjoyed their eight hours of the seaside very heartily and happily. Dignified Brighton, residential Brighton shut itself up on "trippers' days", but it was not to be dislodged. It simply abstained from the sea-front till the "trippers" were gone, and then came out and took long breaths of sea-breeze untainted with stale fuzees and orange peel.'

In order to escape from such horrors the true holidaymaker searched for pastures new, but it was a losing battle. It was not as though the hotels benefited financially to any great extent. There was a cartoon in *Punch* of 1888 showing a stream of trippers leaving a railway station at a seaside resort. A man is talking to the head waiter of an hotel as the crowds stream by. 'What a roaring trade the hotels will be doing with these holiday folk,' remarks the man. The head waiter answers gloomily, 'Lor bless yer, sir, no! They all bring their nosebags with 'em!'

The moral evils of cheap trains were clearly seen by some people. James Farr of Lytham in 1846 expressed such views very strongly to the Preston Wyre Railway Harbour and Dock Company, Fleetwood-on-Wyre, Lancashire, and the assurance he received from H. Bassett Jones, Secretary of the railway company amounted to this: 'I am instructed to assure you that if the evils you anticipate are realised, by the experiment of cheap trains, the subject shall receive the serious attention of the Board with an earnest desire to remove the cause of complaint.'

A disgruntled Francis Kilvert in 1870 complained, 'coming back we met a noisy rabble of tourists, males and females, rushing down the roads towards Land's End as if they meant to break their necks, and no great loss either'.

Samuel Butler was no happier.

'There are Canterbury Pilgrims every Sunday in summer who start from close to the old Tabard, only they go by the South-Eastern Railway and come back the same day for five shillings.

If they do not go to Canterbury they go by the *Clacton Belle* to Clacton-on-Sea. There is not a Sunday the whole summer through but you may find all Chaucer's pilgrims . . . on board the *Lord of the Isles* or the *Clacton Belle*. Why, I have seen the Wife of Bath on the *Lord of the Isles* myself. She was eating her lunch off an *Ally Sloper's Half-Holiday*, which was spread upon her knees . . .'

Again, Kilvert, visiting abbey ruins in Wales described his horror at seeing 'two tourists with staves and shoulder-belts all complete postured among the ruins discussing learnedly to his gaping companion and pointing out objects of interest with his stick'. And in a tirade against tourists in general, Kilvert added, 'and of all tourists the most vulgar, ill bred, offensive and loathsome is the British tourist. No wonder dogs fly at them and consider them vermin to be exterminated.' If possible, there was worse to come. The tourists had arrived at the hotel before Kilvert and his party, and had already ordered dinner. 'So we had to wait till they had done, solacing ourselves with the *Hereford Times* and the Visitors' Book from which to the great and just indignation of the landlord some of the British tourists had cut out and *stolen* half a year of entries from October 1865 to May 1866, including my last entry.'

There was hooliganism and vandalism. In 1885 a church in Essex became so dilapidated due to 'destruction by tourists from London who force an entrance into it, desecrate it, thereby causing great scandal' that the Bishop of St Albans was urged to sell the bricks, pews etc., so that the proceeds should contribute towards the building of a new vicarage.

At a more elevated level the Earl of Shrewsbury had cause to write to Thomas Cook in the 1870s complaining about the disorderly conduct of a party of excursionists from Wednesbury who had come to his estate. 'I am sorry to say,' wrote the Earl, 'there were many of them half drunk when they came, and finished the day in a state of intoxication.' His intention in opening his grounds to the public was, the Earl explained, 'to afford reasonable recreation'. As it was the second offence on the part of Wednesbury excursionists he was compelled to give instructions that no further excursion trains from that district must be sent.

Peak Frean's, the biscuit firm, discontinued their outings after 1857 because of rowdyism, and Huntley & Palmers in 1898 caused their Excursion Committee to print in large red letters an inch high on a poster: A GLASS BOTTLE WAS THROWN FROM ONE OF THE CARRIAGES DURING THE JOURNEY TO RAMSGATE, NEARLY HITTING A PLATELAYER.

In 1891, 900 stevedores visited Southend for the day. When the time came for them to return home, many were drunk. Fighting broke out in the High Street and there were clashes with the police. The *Southend Standard* reported that 'early in the day a man named Bunker was found by the police drunk and incapable. He was conveyed to the station on a stretcher, and during the day was charged before G. D. Deeping, Esq. and fined 2s 6d and 3s 6d costs.'

The inhabitants of the invaded resorts were understandably shaken by such incidents, but voices were heard that urged tolerance. A letter headed 'Health for the Toilers' appeared in the *Southend Standard* of 17 May 1894:

'We hold a proud position as a Borough for we can truly say that the beauties of Southend have aided in brightening at least one day in the clouded lives of masses of London's East End toilers.

'There are some fastidious and unfeeling creatures who don't hesitate to publicly state that poor and dirty people should be shut away from the fresh air, which is only to be inhaled by the kid-glove fraternity . . . We all derive—directly and indirectly— benefit from the money spent in Southend by the crowds of day trippers, so that their welfare is ours. May the influx of these excursions increase by leaps and bounds.

'If any of us have the skill to make the fun go faster let us do our best to add to the jollity. Remember 'Arry and 'Arriet don't laugh and dance every day.

'Forget not that if you can force a smile upon a sad and sickly face you have done *something* for humanity's sake. Welcome the day trippers!'

Even in 1875 the arrival at Southend of 3,000 excursionists from the Clyde Wharf Sugar Refinery in two special trains and five Woolwich steamers caused no disturbance. It was reported that the townspeople 'showed a moderation of civility which the inhabitants of other places of holiday resort would do well to imitate'.

How did the trippers fare abroad? It is worth recording the impression of the French press when in May 1900 1,600 workers from Port Sunlight visited the Universal Exhibition in Paris.

'The weather, like the trip was "Sunlight" from start to finish,' it was recorded in the house journal *Progress*. Each employee who went was insured by the firm to the extent of £100 in case of death, or £2 a week for life in case of total disablement. On arrival in Paris the excursionists were taken through the streets in a cavalcade of vehicles each bearing the notice:

EXCURSION

des Employés de		of the Employees of
	LEVER BROTHERS LTD	
Angleterre	—Port Sunlight—	England
Fabricants du		Manufacturers of
Savon	—SUNLIGHT—	Soap

Their behaviour impressed the French journals. *Figaro* reported

'. . . in groups they pass out of the station in perfect order, without appearing to obey any word of command. No laughing or shouting; each seems to be there on his or her own account, oblivious of those in front or behind. The same absence of unity in dress and deportment. Are these people from town or country? There's no telling. Cheek by jowl with plain apparel are dust coats of immaculate cut; dainty tanned boots walk side by side with shoes that have seen better days. Some walk with hands in their pockets; others carry the plaid and handbag of the elegant tourist; there the sober, spectacled matron hanging on the arm of her dutiful spouse.'

Even when goaded jokingly by a Frenchman who exclaimed with a smile, 'Dirty Ingleesh', the sharp reply came from a loyal Sunlighter, 'Nong, Nong,' she cried indignantly, 'Washy, washy Sunlight savon,' and she mimed the action to the words. The Frenchman, it is reported, roared with laughter.

Until the last quarter of the nineteenth century places on the Lincolnshire coastline, such as Cleethorpes and Skegness, were fishing villages of no significance. Inland villages were agricultural. The railways brought prosperity and people, but at the cost of peace and stability. The Manchester, Sheffield and Lancashire Railway had a prosperous excursion traffic which brought as many as 30,000 people in a single day from the West Riding industrial towns to Cleethorpes. It can be imagined what such an influx did for a place that was unprepared for such an invasion. The *Illustrated Times* in 1857 published a series of articles on the seaside resorts and had these comments to make about Hastings, where there were bands 'discoursing eloquent music from early morn to dewy eve; but there are no amusements, except a few exotics imported. There is no theatre; the corporation, we were told, will not sanction anything so immoral.'

The shopkeepers in the seaside resorts welcomed the visitors as they poured from the trains. Although many visitors may have brought their own 'nosebags', their purchasing power was impressive. The shopkeepers of Deal, for example, were so concerned at not receiving the benefits they felt were due to them from visitors, that in 1888 they petitioned the Mayor and Corporation as follows:

'We, the undersigned, *Tradesmen* Burgesses of the Borough of Deal, beg to submit to your notice that for some reasons the Borough of Deal has been excluded from the cheap daily excursions, which have been extended to other Watering Places on the South Eastern and London to Chatham Railways. We have been entirely isolated from receiving benefits not only by money spent by excursionists but totally ignoring our town, one of the prettiest Watering Places on the Coast of Kent. It may be urged by some, that cheap day excursions do a Watering Place an injury but experience tells us different, judging from other towns where trade is particularly helped in this way.

'It is a well-known fact that, these Wagonettes which ply from the Isle of Thanet to Deal during the Summer, have done the town more good than many advertising mediums.

'Many who have visited Deal in this way had never heard of the Town before and were delighted with the place and have become constant visitors afterwards. The Memorialists would also call the attention of the Council to the two Band of Hope excursions from Maidstone to Deal July 16, 1884, July 15, 1885 both caused plenty of Money to be circulated, the Confectioners, Refreshment Houses, Fruiterers, Fancy dealers doing four times the amount of Business.

'Under the circumstances together with the short seasons we experience, particularly the last two years, we feel convinced it would conduce much to the prosperity of Deal to have the same favours granted by the Railway Companies that have been extended to the Watering Places along the coast . . .'

Ending with 'Your Memorialists will ever pray', the petition was signed by Walter Shorey Coppin, 180a, 180b, High Street, Deal and some 133 other tradesmen.

Another objection was that excursion trains ran on Sundays. 'Remember to keep holy the Sabbath Day' was the banner unfurled by the Church, and the argument that excursionists could and would attend places of worship at the resorts they visited was vigorously countered by the fact that engine drivers, porters, guards had to give up *their* Sundays.

On the one hand there was Dr Arnold who stated that 'Sunday should be a day of greater leisure than other days, and of the suspension, as far as may be, of the common business of life, I quite allow; and . . . if the Railway enables the people in the great towns to get out into the country on a Sunday, I should think it a very great good'. On the other hand the Rev. J. Parker, Minister of the Independent Chapel, Banbury issued a tract in 1856 as follows:

'If we thoroughly knew the history of the Sunday excursionists we should find amongst them the dirtiest, the silliest, the laziest, and the poorest of the toiling population. This may be said of the majority; and if the minority choose such society, let them remember "that a companion of fools shall be destroyed".'

In one of the numerous pamphlets issued in the nineteenth century, two men working in a noisy factory on a hot summer day discuss the issue. One man, Harry, says he does not approve of Sunday excursions but that a day out would 'give the missis and the young-uns a bit of a treat for once in a way. You see, John, we can keep Sunday just as well there as here, because we shall go to a place of worship.'

John replies, 'I consider it selfish in the highest degree, for one class of persons to say to another, "You must forego the boon of a day of rest, and the privilege of attending a place of worship, that we may enjoy ourselves on the Sunday." It is a kind of despotism. It is one class of men making another class slaves on that day when *all* men should be free to rest, and refresh their souls and bodies.'

In the middle of the nineteenth century there appeared an astonishing document* on the subject of Sunday excursion travel. The Archdeacon quotes the experiences of a 'Christian Observer' who reported that

'Thousands, and tens of thousands have been led, during the summer season, to travel by the South Western Railway on the Lord's-day, causing to an awful extent the desecration of the Sabbath, even to such an extent, that the Railway Servants have been kept in a complete state of Sabbath Slavery, bound down to incessant labour. It may truly be said of many of them, that they know not a day of rest. That which is a day of rest and freedom to others, is a day of labour and slavery to them. The very freedom others enjoy, is the cause of their slavery, for during the Sunday, on the South-Western Railway, there are many more travelling than on any other day of the week. I have myself witnessed the awful scene of Sabbath Desecration at the Waterloo Terminus, between the hours of eight and ten in the morning, from three to six o'clock in the afternoon, and from ten to eleven at night.'

The Archdeacon had been assured that no Sunday excursion did or would go out 'from Southampton to disturb the sacred rest! Within six weeks of the assurance,' he thundered, 'I read in the Southampton papers, the advertisement of "a Sunday excursion train to the pleasant village of Bishopstoke!!" ' He had also heard that the 'quiet neighbourhood of Alton . . . had been thoroughly disturbed by the effects of a new excursion train'.

The Archdeacon went on to say that he was told the population of London must have healthful change and recreation on the

* *An Appeal to the Better Feelings of the Managers and Directors of the Railway and Steam-Packet Companies, connected with the Port of Southampton on behalf of their servants, and of the Christian Welfare of the town with extracts from a charge delivered to the clergy and churchwardens of the Archdeaconry of Winchester in April 1853 by Joseph C. Wigram, Archdeacon and Rector of St. Mary's Southampton.* Printed at the Operative Jewish Converts' Institution.

Lord's Day. 'If this be the object of excursion trains,' continued
the Archdeacon

'we may draw from the assertion an argument, not in favour perhaps of changing the air, but at least of giving the respite of a
seventh-day rest to the mechanics, who are employed all week in
our ships and docks! But, then, if this be the purpose of excursion
trains, it is quite unnecessary that there should be *above twenty*
trains in and out of Southampton on the Lord's-day; it is utterly
needless, that carriages should go out for such purpose from any
towns, where the people are NOT *pent up*; and still more so, that
trains should run on that day from country places into the
metropolis itself.'

As early as 1839 the Ulster Railway Company wanted to run
trains on Sunday except between eleven and twelve in the morning
when the excursionists were expected to be in church, but at a
half-yearly meeting the motion was defeated by a large majority.
Excursionists were mostly clerks, warehousemen 'and the decenter
sort of operatives, with some females and children'. On one
occasion 'the day passed off without the least irregularity or
disturbance, and not a small proportion of visitors attended service
in the afternoon at church'.

In 1835 leading figures in the religious life of the community
prevailed upon the Hull and Selby Railway to include in their
Bill for permission to build a line a clause preventing all Sunday
trains, but when the Bill came before the Commons the clause
was struck out and a petition on behalf of the Methodists of Hull
for its re-introduction was rejected. Trains were run on a Sunday
but the Board of the Railway Company, determined to put a stop
to it, passed a resolution 'forbidding excursions of mere pleasure
leading inevitably to most extensive desecration of the Lord's Day
and consequent general dissipation to the manifest injury of all
quiet and good order in our town', and until the line was leased to
an individual, the Hull and Selby was outstanding in the north-
east region for its opposition to unnecessary Sunday trains.

In an attempt to dissuade people of Newcastle from joining an
excursion in August 1841, the Rev. W. C. Burns of Kilsyth issued
a handbill entitled 'A Reward for Sabbath Breaking' implying that
Hell might be the eventual destination for those taking the trip.

The National Sunday League was formed in 1855 'to promote the Opening of the British Museum, National Gallery, Crystal Palace, and similar Institutions on Sunday Afternoon'.* During the summer months the League undertook to run cheap Sunday excursions so 'that the Country and the Sea-side may be visited by the week-day Toilers of the Metropolis on their day of rest'.

In the late 1860s and thereafter Sunday excursions were organised to Ramsgate, St Leonards, Hastings, Brighton, Box Hill and Dorking. There were trips to Hampton Court and Southend by steamer, the latter 'having enjoyed a reputation for good and cheap Refreshments; we trust the caterers will continue to sustain it, and not plead "high price of coals" as a excuse for putting on 50 per cent'. Reasons for raising prices have not changed over the years.

In about 1885 a Sunday excursion was arranged by the League leaving London Bridge and Victoria on the London, Brighton & South Coast Railway for Arundel and Littlehampton. 'The Morning may be passed at Littlehampton by the Sea-side, and trains will leave there at 2.30 for Arundel (free of charge). The Arundel Band will play a selection of Music during the Evening in the Duke of Norfolk's magnificent Park.' The excursionists returned to London at 7 pm and the return fare was 3s 6d for adults; 2s for children.

The League fought battles to achieve their objectives and the following revealing advertisement appeared in the September 1856 issue of their journal, the *National Sunday Record*:

'ONE HUNDRED POUNDS offered!
'I am ready to give the above sum to any person who shall prove, from the Old or New Testament only: First, That I am, as a Christian, bound to keep a Sabbath-day, as the Jews were; and Secondly, that Sunday, the first day of the week, is the day I am so bound to keep.

'I admit the obligation on Christians to meet on the first day of the week (Hcb. x. 25), but with that proviso I deny that I am forbid doing anything on it I might lawfully do on any other day.

* A few months later the League's objectives were expanded to include all public museums, galleries, libraries and gardens in the towns of England, Scotland and Ireland 'for the Instruction, Recreation and Innocent Amusement of the Working Class'.

My name and address, for *bona fide* inquirers, I leave with the Editor.'

There is no indication that the challenge was taken up.

On a Sunday excursion from Dudley to Hayley and Clent Hills in 1858 the party was accompanied by musicians. At Hayley Park, the seat of Lord Lyttleton the music was too tempting to resist. 'Two or three of the young folks resolved to beat time on the light fantastic', but a tenant of his Lordship appeared and said that if his Lordship knew that there had been dancing on a Sunday it would mean instant dismissal and that he (the tenant) 'might be turned adrift at a day's notice'. The account ends: 'This being the case, and his Lordship not being a member of the Sunday League, the young folks promised to desist . . .'

During the year 1913–1914 540 Sunday excursions took place, and between the wars greater distances were travelled at incredibly low prices as many living to-day will testify.

In 1898 The Anti-Sunday Travelling Union claimed a membership of over 20,000, but by 1913 at a shareholders' meeting of the London and North Western Railway a leading Sabbatarian had to abandon his speech against Sunday excursions because of shouts and threats to throw him out. The general view of the meeting was that Sunday excursions were 'works of charity and necessity' as they gave workpeople from the overcrowded cities an opportunity to breathe clean, fresh air. Surely such experience could lead to a greater faith in God than would be achieved by attendance at church?

Although travelling by train should have been a pleasurable pastime there was, in the public's mind, a suspicion that railways were unsafe, uncomfortable (and this was not confined to third-class travel), unreliable, and that plunging into tunnels at twenty or thirty miles an hour was bad for health, but a medical man of eminence at that time described the difference between the stage coach and the railway carriage. The latter 'equalizes the circulation, promotes digestion, tranquilizes the nerves, and often causes sleep during the succeeding night . . .' In the opinion of a lady living in London in the 1870s excursion trains were all that were horrible. 'Long and unearthly hours, packed carriages, queer company, continual shuntings aside and waiting for regular trains to go by,

and worst of all the contempt of decent travellers.' She remembers
a venomous little rhyme which ended:

> Grown old and rusted, the boiler busted
> And smashed the excursion train.

So much for the upper-class point of view, but the excursion
train was seen in a different light by the working classes. A miner,
one of a party of 850 on an excursion to Hull from the collieries at
North Gawber near Barnsley and surroundings considered the
excursion train had a different message, and conveyed it as verse:

> The monster he puff'd, gave a whistle—a scream—
> Then belched from its nostrils a volume of steam;
> And seem'd to say—'Follow me, I will lead on,
> And take you just now to the garden of Eden.'

Tunnels were unpleasant, especially when most of the carriages
were open and it is evident that passengers required reassurance
about them which Arthur Freeling, in his *Picturesque Excursions*,
published in 1839, was prepared to give. The jaunt mentioned was
from Shoreham to Brighton and the first-class fare was 1s; 2nd
class 9d and 3rd class 3d. 'Railway travelling being now the most
important mode of migration,' begins Mr Freeling, 'we shall
commence . . . with a jaunt per railway to Shoreham . . . Proceed
we to the Railway; and having taken our places the signal is given,
and we start; passing through the Tunnel at New England, we
find ourselves in the fields near Hove.' A light-hearted attempt to
describe most people's feelings towards tunnels was written in
verse by J. Bradshawe Walker and published in 1845 in the *Handbook of the Trip to Liverpool* compiled by Thomas Cook.

> THE TUNNEL GLEE
> Bright day, farewell
> 'Tis darkness all,
> We're out of call;
> And who can tell
> Of the wondrous things,
> On feet, or on wings,
> That are overhead—
> The living and the dead;
> Or what hidden store,

From the floor, or before,
Lies darkling around,
Deep, deep in the ground?
High hills o'er us
We pant for the night.
Away! away!
All hail, bright day!

The excursion scene was not for the upper classes, but the artisans, anxious to get away from the cities, enjoyed the companionship of their own kind on what was likely to be a hazardous expedition and certainly an uncomfortable one. Dangers and discomforts shared could transform the situation for the better.

There is little doubt that the running of the excursion trains in addition to the normal traffic put considerable strain on the railway staff who were expected to work all the hours that were necessary. Compulsory rest periods were not legislated for, as this announcement by the Lancashire and Yorkshire Railway to staff for the 1871 Whitsun holiday indicates: 'It is earnestly requested that, as many of the Guards and Enginemen will have to make long hours during Whit-week they will take as much rest as they can during the day.'

The growth of the railway system had been massive, much money had been sunk in ventures and quick financial returns were looked for. The directors of the railway companies were the objects of criticism, particularly from *Punch*. The directors, it was said, had only one interest, which was making money. They had not the slightest concern for the comfort of passengers or the disruptions in the service, and they were equally negligent about standards of safety. Henry Mayhew and George Cruikshank complained, in 1851, about the youthfulness of the station staff on the Cockermouth to Workington line which was much used for excursion traffic. The line

'being in none of the most flourishing conditions, every means for economizing the "working expenses" have been resorted to. The men engaged upon it have been cut down to boys; so that the establishment has very much the look of a kind of railway academy, where the porters on the platform are ever playing at marbles or leapfrog ... We *have* heard the united ages of the entire staff, but fear to mention the small amount, lest a too incredulous public should accuse us of magnifying, or rather parvifying the tenderness of their years. Suffice it is that not a razor is used by the whole establishment; and that the "staff"— we have it on the best authority—are allowed to give over work an hour earlier Saturday evening, in consideration of it being "tub-night".'

Railway workers were poorly paid and it was cheaper to use them for safety precautions than to indulge in mechanical aids. The Lancashire and Yorkshire Railway's train arrangements for Whitsun 1871 also indicates how much safety depended on the human being.

'On Whit Monday and Tuesday, Platelayers will be stationed along the line between Blackburn and Preston about every half mile distant, to signal the specials in the event of their approaching too near each other, both going and returning. Drivers must therefore keep a good look-out for any signals they may give, with a view to ensure safety.'

As early as 1844 the dangers to passengers in trains of numerous coaches sometimes of unmanageable proportions were realised by the Board of Trade which, in a circular for the 'Attention of the Lords of the Committee of Privy Council for Trade' stated,

'My Lords desire that it may be clearly understood, that they by no means wish to suppress excursions ... but my Lords are most anxious that their very utility, and consequent magnitude, should not lead to the disastrous result which must ensue, if the practice of conveying great multitudes along railways be not accompanied by a better system than that which hitherto prevailed.'

The crowds of people waiting for excursion trains on platforms were sometimes in potential danger. In 1847 excursionists at Hadleigh Station, awaiting their train for Ipswich, were engulfed in bricks when about 300 feet of new wall, erected at the end of the station, was blown down on them. There were no casualties. At the Elephant and Castle Station in London some forty years later, where about 500 men, women and children were waiting for the excursion train, so great was the rush for the carriages that a man was thrown down and crushed to death between the wheels of the train. The *Illustrated London News* in May 1872 thought that excursionists should and could co-operate more:

'. . . an interesting sight to watch the gathering of pilgrims in quest of harmless and healthy pleasure . . . the process of getting

Shrewsbury & Chester
RAILWAY.

CHEAP TRIP TO
LLANGOLLEN.

On *MONDAY* next, *AUGUST* 2nd, 1852,
A SPECIAL TRAIN

Will leave Shrewsbury at 8 30 a.m. for Llangollen Road Station, where Boats will be in attendance to convey the Excursionists to the Town of Llangollen.

The Boats will leave Llangollen for the Station punctually at 6 0 p.m. and the Train will arrive at Shrewsbury about 9 0 p.m.

Excursionists will therefore have seven clear hours in Llangollen, being sufficient time for visiting most if not all of the following places of attraction, namely Plas Newydd, Casttell Dinas Bran, Vale Crucis Abbey, Pont Cysylltau Aqueduct.

The proceeds of this Train will be given to the Widow and Family of the late John Stanley, who was accidentally killed on the above line of Railway while in the performance of his duties.

An early application for Tickets will be necessary to ensure ample accommodation.

Fare in Covered Carriages, including the charge for Boats, Two Shillings and Sixpence.

Tickets may be obtained of Mr. Howard and Mr. Macdonnell, at the Company's Engine Sheds; Mr. Richard Davies, Printer, 7. High Street, and at the Booking Offices, Shrewsbury Station.
Chester, July 26th, 1852.

their tickets ... is apt to be a little tedious. It would be got through in less than half the time ... if each traveller would first ascertain ... exactly what he or she will have to pay, and would then take out of his or her portemonnaie the shillings and six-penses required ... Ladies who have to extract the sum demanded from a deep pocket or reticule ... while grievously encumbered with a parasol, a veil, a parcel of sweets, biscuits, a camp stool, a black leather bag, and the skirts of the dress and petticoat, seem to be worthy objects of compassion. But nobody can help an un-protected female under the circumstances, for how can the stranger expect to be trusted?'

On a Saturday in October 1869 four excursion trains carrying over 4,000 passengers left Leicester for the Nottingham Goose Fair. It was a dark, foggy night and near Trent Junction there was a collision with a mail train. Eight people died and at the burial service one poor woman who had lost a relative was so over-whelmed with grief that, according to a contemporary source, the service was temporarily interrupted, 'her sobs preventing the clergyman from proceeding with his sad duties'.

On August bank holiday 1876 an excursion train from Bath and a relief train from Wimbourne met in a head-on collision in which twelve passengers were killed and twenty-eight injured, as well as six members of the railway staff. A year later an express ran into the back of an excursion train filled with racegoers. This was at Hexthorpe, hear Doncaster, and twenty-five were killed and ninety-four injured; but the greatest horror of all was on 12 June 1889 on the Newry and Armagh line which involved an excursion train and the loss of eighty lives, many of them children, and very many more injured.

Despite the dangers and discomforts nothing was going to prevent the masses enjoying their new-found freedom. And while on the subject of accidents perhaps we should give the last word to an old coachman who gave a clear distinction between rail and horse coach accidents. 'If,' said he, 'you get comfortably capsized in a ditch by the roadside, there you are! But if you gets blown up by an engine, run into a cutting, or off an embankment, where are you?'

3

The Firm's Annual Outing
1836–1914

'The annual custom, which some people question the good arising from . . . of master and man uniting once a year and going forth from the turmoils of business to enjoy the pure air of heaven . . .'
Leicester Guardian, August 1863

It was the day of the small firm, the family business. The boss spent his money on giving his employees a day outing. This would probably take place on a Saturday—a half-working day, so that there would be a minimum loss of productivity. From the employees' point of view such an outing was constricting in some respects. The boss was present, perhaps with his wife and family. Behaviour was watched, attitudes observed and taken note of. The social divisions were marked. A few tongue-tied words with the boss and the humble employee was glad to retreat to the comparative safety of his own kind. The boss did his best to unbend, and some were better at it than others. His employees might think him a proper bastard on the shop-floor, and no less a bastard on a day outing. On the other hand it was possible that the boss was revealed in a new and better light on such a social occasion.

Workpeople had two kinds of clothing; for work and for 'best'. An outing was an occasion for looking one's best. Hats and smart dresses for the ladies; boaters, homburgs, bowlers, suits and waistcoats for the men. There was no leisure wear as we know it to-day, and how could there be when there was virtually no leisure?

Unlike to-day, when people dress to please themselves, the

Victorians dressed for an occasion out of deference to their host. A day outing was at the invitation of the boss, who had complete control over one's destiny. He had the power to fire you and hire someone else. In common parlance it was important that your face should fit. Additionally it mattered how one appeared before colleagues. On this one occasion in the year they could be seen out of their working clothes, and their 'best' could be most instructive and a subject for discussion during the long working days to follow.

However unbearable glad rags might be on a hot summer day, it was necessary to conform. Stiff collars might go limp with the heat, corsets could stifle, and although there might be opportunities to undo the former and loosen the latter on the way home, it was necessary to appear respectable during the day. There was Sunday in which to recover, but there was always Monday and yet another working week.

In 1836 Mr Barnes, a cotton spinner at Farnworth near Bolton, wished to take some 300 of his employees from Bolton to Liverpool and back for a single fare of 4s, a proposal which officials of the Bolton and Kenyon Railway received with some degree of hesitation. After consultations, a special train was made available and the employees left at 6 a.m. for Liverpool, from where they were conveyed by steamer across to Birkenhead, 'where a delightful day was spent'.

On a Saturday in 1844 Mr Paley treated 650 of his employees—men, women, boys and girls—with seventy of their friends and acquaintances to a pleasure trip from Preston to Fleetwood. Early in the morning they assembled in the factory yard from where, accompanied by a Church of England band, they marched in processional order to the Midland Station. Two royal standards, several flags and union jacks were carried in the procession, and attached to the sides of the train's carriages were a variety of loyal messages and expressive mottoes. On arrival at Fleetwood the day was spent in jollification and two trips were made round the Screw Pile Lighthouse in a steamer at a charge of 6d each. Before returning to Preston about 200 buns were distributed among the children. Arriving back at Preston the excursionists formed a procession, once more following the route March Lane, up Bow Lane, up Fishergate (where three hearty cheers were given as the procession passed Mr Paley's house), down Lune Lane to the factory in Wharf Street where all went their various ways 'delighted with the treat which the charitable bounty of their employer had afforded them'.

The Crystal Palace was still a great novelty three years after it had been erected at Sydenham, and in September 1857 the Palmer brothers (of Huntley & Palmers) paid for a special train to take employees there. The outing was free—and that included tea for 450 people—but rail tickets had to be bought for friends of employees and wives. The event was so successful that the occasion was repeated in 1859, 1866 and 1886, by which time the number taken on the outing had increased to 1,530. The same firm, between 1886 and 1871, went on excursions by rail from Reading to Hampton Court, Brighton (twice), Portsmouth, Southampton and Hastings. Only those employees who had subscribed a penny a week into an excursion fund were allowed to go, but that was their only commitment. The firm paid all other expenses, although dependants of employees usually had to buy their own rail tickets.

Colmans of Norwich held a Whit-week fête in two fields adjacent to Carrow Abbey. At the first fête in 1859 860 people attended. By 1870 the attendance was 3,500. Carpenters started work about a week beforehand, building a wooden bridge over a strip of plantation dividing the two meadows. This was done so that everybody could reach the second meadow for tea. Admission tickets were white and green, and each was divided in half. On one side of each ticket the word TEA was printed. On the other side of the white ticket GINGER BEER, and on the other side of the green ticket, BEER. All the visitors had tea, but they could choose between the other two drinks. Those who came dressed in their Sunday best; each man was handed an ounce of tobacco and a new pipe on entering the grounds.

The tea consisted of ham sandwiches, bread and butter, seed and currant cake. The tea itself was made stronger than at home, as one man pointed out. The ham for the sandwiches was smoked and came from the pig-killing the Christmas before.

The Carrow Works' Band was in attendance and played 'grace' for which everyone stood. There was dancing and kiss-in-the-ring, and the children watched the deer in the Abbey estate. As employees could bring their husbands, wives and families the crowds became so vast that the event had to be discontinued in 1877.

Outings generated considerable expressions of loyalty towards the heads of firms giving them. A day—or even half a day—off work was something to be cherished. If you were ill or had to be away for some reason it was unlikely that you would be paid, and although the cynical might say that employees knew on which side their bread was buttered and it cost nothing to make the right noises in praise of the boss, it seems likely that employees were grateful and that although the gratitude may have appeared fulsome at times, it was often genuine enough. An example is the following resolution by the employees of Chance Bros.:

'RESOLUTION OF THANKS TO MESSRS CHANCE
from the Managers and Workpeople of the Glass Works.

'At a meeting of the Managers and Foreman of Departments of Messrs. Chance Brothers and Company's Glass Works, held on Wednesday, the 17th September 1862, Mr. E. Forster in the Chair, it was unanimously resolved:

'THAT the Managers and others now present, whose names are hereto appended, desire hereby in the names and on behalf of themselves and the Workpeople in their respective Departments respectfully and cordially to express to Messrs. Chance Brothers and Company their strong sense of, and their gratitude for, the very great kindness and liberality recently exhibited towards them by Messrs. Chance, in according to them the opportunity and the means of visiting the International Exhibition; the number conveyed thither and back Free of Charge being 1232.

'And they venture further to express a hope that the visit thus paid to that Wonderful Exposition of the Artistic and Industrial Productions of the World will incite them, one and all, to aid steadily in the development of the progress of the above named Great Establishment, with which their own interests are so closely united, so that the high character of its varied productions may be maintained in any future Exhibitions.'

The address was signed by the Edward Forster mentioned and by twenty-seven employees.

But, as the *Leicester Guardian* of August 1863 pointed out, some people question the good arising from the annual custom of man and master 'uniting once a year, and going forth from the turmoils of business to enjoy the pure air of heaven', although this did not apply to the 'treat' for the workpeople of Messrs Faire, Brother & Porter

'when as happy a gathering as ever left the chimneys of Leicester behind them, met in Belvoir Street, and, headed by the Temperance Brass Band, and with flags and banners waving, and with a clear blue sky, and bright sun shining overhead, wended their way to that charming locality—Bradgate Park, the privilege of entering which everyone ought deeply and sincerely to appreciate.'

In the park a tent was erected, tables placed therein which were 'soon spread with the good things of life under the direction of Mrs. W. L. Faire and Mrs. Henry Porter and these ladies, together with the members of the firm with kind words and smiling faces, invited all to partake'.

After a day spent in the park, the party returned to Leicester, where the streets were thronged with thousands of people. It was 10 p.m. when the vehicles arrived back at the factory in Willow Street where a room had been prepared for further entertainment. Visitors arrived from London, Derby, Sudbury, Market Harborough and Birmingham and the programme of entertainment included a polka; quadrille; song 'Still So Gently' (sung by Mr Hickman, who had been run out for 1 in the cricket match played at Bradgate Park); waltz; recitation, 'The Slave' (Mr G. R. Faire —encored); comic song, 'Dark Girl Dressed in Blue' (Mr J. Louis Faire—encored); caledonians; galop; comic recitation, 'The Countryman and Sergeant' (Mr A. Moulds—encored); polka; performance on the Trapeze (Mr Mousley); Exhibition Overture by the Band, and finally a Country Dance.

In the middle of the programme there were speeches. Mr Mousley rose to thank members of the firm of Faire, Brothers and Porter for their bounteous hospitality during the day. It had been a rich treat to all who had partaken of it. Thanks were due not only to the gentlemen of the firm, but heartfelt thanks were also due to the ladies for the kind attention they had so pleasingly and so admirably shown. He continued, 'I have been in their employ fourteen months and, during that time I have been treated with that kindness and consideration which is sure ever to command respect and esteem, and I believe the same kindness has been paid

GRAND PIC-NIC DAY
AT ASHBY-DE-LA-ZOUCH.

MONDAY NEXT, JUNE 3, 1850,

A SPECIAL TRAIN

WILL LEAVE LEICESTER,

At 9 a.m.; RETURNING from ASHBY at 7-30. Passengers may be taken up and set down at
DESFORD and BAGWORTH.

FARES THERE AND BACK: FIRST CLASS, 3s. 6d.; COVERED CARRIAGES, 2s.

This being the first Pleasure Trip to Ashby since the opening of the Railway, the inhabitants are preparing to give the visitors a hearty welcome, and a Committee, consisting of some of the principal gentlemen of the town, is formed for the purpose of arranging and superintending the festive proceedings. It is expected that business will be generally suspended and the day devoted to mutual pleasureable intercourse.
Every facility will be given for viewing the various places and objects of interest in the town and its immediate locality.

THE

Ivanhoe Baths & Royal Hotel

With the extensive range of Pleasure Grounds adjoining, will be thrown open to the Visitors.

THE CASTLE AND PLEASURE GROUNDS

Surrounding, will also be opened for a free inspection and promenade. The arrangements will provide for a variety of

POPULAR AMUSEMENTS,

Including CRICKET, ARCHERY, SKITTLES, QUOITS, &c., and one or more

QUADRILLE BANDS

Will be engaged for the accommodation of DANCING PARTIES on the Grounds of the Baths and Castle.

TWO POWERFUL BRASS BANDS

Are also engaged, one of which, provided by Mr. H. NICHOLSON, of Leicester,—principal Cornet-à-Piston, Mr. J. SMITH,—will accompany the Train, and will perform at the Baths. The MELBOURN BAND is engaged by Mr. MILLS, of the Queen's Hotel, and will perform at the Castle.

THE BATHS will be at the service of those who choose to bathe at the reduced charge of 6d. to the warm fresh water bath, and the salt water baths at very reduced rates.

By the kindness and courtesy of SIR GEORGE BEAUMONT, Bart.,

THE GARDENS AND GROUNDS OF COLEORTON HALL,

Distant about two miles from Ashby, will be opened for the gratification of visitors by the Special Train, on shewing their Tickets; and the Hotel and Coach Proprietors of Ashby have liberally arranged for Omnibuses and other conveyances to ply to and fro at intervals during the day, by which parties will be conveyed at the nominal charge of 6d. each. The Winter and Italian Gardens are celebrated for their beauty and taste. Wordsworth, the late Poet Laureate, thus wrote in his dedication of "The Anniversary" for 1849, to the late Sir George Beaumont:—

"Several of my best poems were composed under the shade of your own groves—upon the classic ground of Coleorton—where I was animated by the recollection of those illustrious poets of your name and family, who were born in that neighbourhood: and we may be assured, did not wander with indifference by the dashing stream of Gracedieu, and among the rocks that diversify the forest of Charnwood. Nor is there any one to whom such parts of this collection as have been inspired or colored by the beautiful country from which I now address you, could be presented with more propriety than to yourself, who have composed so many admirable pictures from the suggestions of the same scenery"

Visitors will be conducted through the Gardens by Mr. Henderson, the head gardener, and it is confidently hoped that the great liberality of the noble proprietor will not in the slightest degree be abused by any act of damage or indecorum. Visitors are especially requested not to pluck flowers or handle the statues, &c.

THE PRINCIPAL HOTEL PROPRIETORS, vieing with the other respectable inhabitants in their desires to contribute to the comfort and pleasure of the visitors, have agreed to provide REFRESHMENTS on the following liberal terms:—COLD COLLATIONS, to be available from 12 till 2 o'clock, 1s. each person, (drinks excepted); TEA, from 5 to 7 o'clock, 1s. each. Mr. Beavington, of the Royal Hotel, will furnish tables in the Bath Rooms, and has engaged the Splendid Tea Apparatus of the Leicester Temperance Society, which will be fitted up under the collonade of the Ivanhoe Baths; Mr. Mills, of the Queen's Hotel, will fit up a booth for Tea and other Refreshments, on the castle grounds; and Mr. Usherwood, of the Saracen's Head, and Mr. Sutton, of the Lamb Hotel, will also erect booths on their respective grounds for the accommodation of visitors.
The feelings, views, and predjudices of all classes will be properly consulted, and it is the earnest desire of the Committee that all may blend in harmonious efforts to facilitate the pleasure of the whole.

TICKETS for the Special Train may be had at the Desford and Bagworth Stations, and of the Manager of the Trip,

T. COOK, 28, Granby-street, Leicester.

N. B.—As a matter of convenience to the Railway Company, it is earnestly requested that parties will secure their Tickets by Saturday night

T. COOK, PRINTER, 28, GRANBY-STREET, LEICESTER.

to every person in their employment.' Mr Mousley concluded his speech in similar vein and the toast was drunk with musical honours.

Mr W. L. Faire, the senior partner then rose to reply. 'I rise with deep emotion,' he said, 'to acknowledge the vote of thanks awarded to myself and partners. I can assure you that in getting up this holiday our only desire has been to make you all happy ... If we take the many smiling faces we have gazed upon to-day as a criterion I think we may safely conclude that you all had a jolly day of it.'

An insight into the financing of outings and the lengths the railway companies were prepared to go to get custom is shown by the following letter from the General Superintendent's Office, Caledonian Company, Buchanan Street Station, Glasgow. It is dated 21 June 1870 and addressed to Robert Hodge, Esq., Cummersdale Printing Works, near Carlisle. The writer apologises for an error that has been made in quoting a rate for an outing, due to the fact that he was in London and did not attend to the matter himself.

'If not too late, I shall be glad to enter into arrangements with your party to carry them to Edinburgh, and back with permission for those who wish to do so, to go to Lanark for the Falls of Clyde, instead of Edinburgh, taking the whole of the three hundred full fares are guaranteed—at 4s for each Adult—children half fare—Also provided you make no addition to the charge to the individuals beyond the 4s charged by the Company I will allow you 7% discount on the gross receipts. A Band, if in Uniform, will be carried at half of the above fare, and a First Class Carriage shall be at the service of the Committee at second class fares.'

Every firm has its 'character'—eccentric, loyal, spreader of gossip and knowledgeable to such a degree about the firm's affairs that he should obviously be running the business. Such a character must have been Tommy Green whose escapades on an outing from Carlisle to Buttermere on 5 August 1871 are recorded in verse by Jimmy Dyer. He tells a sad story of Tommy's fall from grace. The 'upper ten' referred to must have been the élite foremen of the factory:

Tommy's get up was extensive, he'd on a blue chinty vest,
His deceased pony's curb chain adorned his manly breast.

Also a pocket-pistol already might be seen,
Loaded with a pint of rum to inspire Tommy Green.

A party of our 'upper ten' did a wagonette prepare
To take a drive through Borrowdale to famous Buttermere
And view the various beauties that along the route is seen
And to provide themselves with music they carried Tommy Green.

To go in such high company made Tommy feel quite proud,
And songs in praise of Cummersdale he sang both long and loud,
Which caused no small sensation where'eer their trap was seen,
Folks thought they had caught a 'queer fish' when they saw Tommy
    Green.

So he brought them more attention than our travellers did desire
And to throw poor Tommy overboard they quickly did conspire.
He begged hard to go on, but no pity was there seen
And like Crusoe on his island they abandoned Tommy Green.

'O! Let me go,' cried Tommy Green, 'only let me go with you,
And I'll sing or I'll be silent, and anything I'll do.'
But they only drove the faster. Tommy did not feel serene
While the echoing hills of Borrowdale only answered Tommy Green.

Tommy drowns his sorrows with rum—from the pocket pistol
presumably—and up comes another trap which takes him on
board.

Then up spake a good templar 'with us you may come in
If you'll "throw away the bottle" for drinking is a sin.'
Poor Tommy sent it flying and it no more was seen,
A bottle when it's empty is not much use to Tommy Green.

Then Tommy sadly mounted up each one tried him to cheer,
But the old man's heart was broken by the trip to Buttermere.
It would have touched the hardest heart his sorrow to have seen
And Honister Crag near melted at the sight of Tommy Green.

Stead, McAlpine, calico printers of Carlisle whose outing it was
that inspired the above verse, had something of a tradition for
rhyming descriptions. The next one concerns an outing to Cummersdale on 5 August 1876 and is written by one of the participants.
The poet laments the lack of business in August when customers
leave town on pleasure bent and orders are small and scarce; in
short 'when things are bad'. Despite the glories of the countryside

the only thing that really matters is the Hamper containing the
food and drink.

> At such a time just once a year
> We make a trip, our hearts to cheer
> To enjoy a little change of scene
> And make a break in life's routine
> Our drooping spirits just to raise
> Till the return of better days . . .
> This year we tried the Midland Line
> Through eden's vale, the English Rhine . . .
> The Glass had foretold a glorious day
> And soon has broke the morning gray
> From Cummersdale, Blackwell, Upperby and Town
> Trippers all stationward coming rushing down
> All eager with their friends to meet
> And be in time to get a seat . . .

The poet continues:

> And though no luggage was allowed
> A full Hamper's carried through the crowd
> Which a well-known label bare
> Glass, this side up with care.
> The porters much to their relief
> Delivered it unto the chief
> Who very quickly did prepare
> To stow it by with ceremonious care . . .
> But as the train went on its way
> It well the traveller did repay
> With the sight of many a lovely dell
> Wild lonely moor, and lofty fell
> And wooded groves by eden's stream
> That in the morning sun did gleam
> But the finest sight along the route
> Was when the Hamper was brought out
> And a glass was raised to every lip
> To drink to Cummersdale and the Trip
> A day like this does surely make amends
> Here's the next toast, our absent friends.

And the final couplet:

> The distance to some may prove a damper
> But only let them try it with a Hamper.

Mr Edward Ecroyd, in August 1881, permitted about 1,200 employees of his firm, Wm. Ecroyd & Sons, Lomeshaye Mills, to visit the ample grounds of his home at Armathwaite in Cumberland.

Thirty-nine Captains were appointed for maintaining order and punctuality. Employees were requested to be courteous and of good behaviour 'to promote and comfort and well-being of the rest.' Care had to be taken not to damage fences, pluck garden flowers, fruits or ferns 'or do any mischief'. Young people were urged to show deference and respect to those more advanced in years.

The employees left Nelson at 5.15 in the morning and on arrival at Armathwaite were given tea or coffee and a bun. For lunch at one o'clock there was meat pie and beer or ginger beer in the Field or Tent. From a local newspaper account of the event it seems 'the [lunch] provision fell somewhat short of the requirement; but roast beef and cold pies were brought from the mansions and under the dextrous carving of Mr. Ecroyd, the deficit was amply and speedily made up'.

The weather was fine, 'a small choir sang a hymn very nicely in the centre of the village' and there was, for the young people, dancing to the music played by the Nelson Prize Band. The programme of dance music included Sir Roger de Coverley, polka, schottische, quadrille, waltz, lancers etc. There was cricket, rounders and other games in the Pasture Fields and Mown Meadows, and boating on the Eden under the supervision of the Captains.

The local newspaper pointed out 'how hearty, happy and healthy the party looked as a whole. One saw very few of the pale, spent faces that one usually expects in a crowd of mill workers'. Mr Ecroyd made a lengthy speech in praise of the firm, his co-directors, employees and God, and the benefits that worship bestowed on the faithful. ('Aye, we know it,' came the response.) Before the party left for home at six o'clock there was tea and a bun for each of the visitors.

Leaving London at 8.30 a.m. on Saturday, 28 June 1890, the employees of S. Z. de Ferranti visited Brighton for a Programme of Sports on the occasion of the Annual Beanfeast. In addition to the conventional 100-yards, 440-yards and one-mile races, events included Throwing the Cricket Ball, Sack Race, Long Pipe Race, Egg and Spoon Race. Dinner was on the table at '1.15 sharp' at Green's, 37 West Street, Brighton and the employees sat down to this menu:

> Roast Beef
> Fore-quarter of Lamb—*Mint Sauce*
> Roast Fowl and Ham—*Seasoning*
> Roast Duck—*Stuffing*
> Boiled Beef and Carrots
> Roast Leg of Mutton
> Roast Veal and Ham—*Seasoning*
> Potatoes, Summer Greens, Green Peas, French Beans
> Pastry—*three sorts*
> Cheese.   Salad.

During the lunch there were Selections by the Band. The sporting events presumably took place after lunch, but with what success can only be imagined. The train left Brighton for London at 8.40 p.m.

Catering was an important and profitable business with so many firms arriving at the seaside resorts. The success of an outing depended on the food and some local newspapers such as the *Hastings & St Leonard's Weekly Mail and Times* included an editorial paragraph about the catering firms and the excursionists they fed. In the issue of 25 June 1904 it was revealed that Messrs Atkins Bros. & Co. (known locally as 'Messrs A.B.C.') had catered for employees visiting Hastings from the Home & Colonial Stores, The Mazawattee Tea Company, and a party of Birkhamstead [sic] brewers.

The Diamond Jubilee of Queen Victoria in 1897 was the occasion for many excursions to London. Two thousand three hundred —the complete office and works staff (except those under 18)—of Lever Bros at Port Sunlight boarded six special trains at about 4 a.m., arriving at Euston between 9 and 10. Some had never been to London before and they toured the city in brakes and private buses. Stops were made at the Houses of Parliament, St Paul's and other places of interest, and according to the *Morning Leader* of the day, 'the drivers of the various conveyances were observed to be enjoying the situation immensely, pointing out to pretty Lancashire lasses the wonderful things on every side, and ready with a fictitious anecdote for each public building'. The journal also reminded its readers that 'although the expense of the outing was tremendous, each employee will be paid his or her usual wages without the deduction of a penny'. The party left London for Birkenhead between 7.30 and 8 p.m.

Blackie & Son Ltd organised a Complimentary Excursion for their employees from Glasgow (Villafield Works) to Killin on 11 June 1904. A special train left Buchanan Street No. 2 Platform at 7.30 a.m. which was due at Killin at 10.20. On arrival refreshments with milk were supplied and during the day a Grand Musical Entertainment was given.

Part Song:	'Ye Mariners of England'	Choir
Song:	'Sound the Pibroch'	Miss M'Coll
Part Song:	'Ye Banks and Braes'	Choir
Solo Dance:	Highland Fling	Mr J. McLean
Part Song:	'Hail to the Chief'	Choir

VOTE OF THANKS

Solo Dance:	'Shean Trews'	Miss C. Lawson
Part Song:	'Hail, Smiling Morn!'	Choir
Song:	'I lo'e nae a Laddie'	Miss Renwick
Part Song:	'Scots Wha Hae'	Choir
Song:	Selected	Mr Fraser
Reading:	Selected	Mr J. McLean
Song:	'Will ye no' come back again?'	Miss Coggan & Choir

AULD LANG SYNE

Afternoon tea was served from three until four-thirty and W. H. Cole's orchestra, which accompanied the excursion, played appropriate music for dancing. It was pointed out that papers and rubbish should be put into the boxes provided for the purpose and not thrown on the field, and those who wished to climb the hills should go through the gates and not climb over the fences. The train returning to Glasgow left Killin at 5 p.m. arriving at Buchanan Street at 7.25 p.m.

Later in the month Dr Blackie received a letter:

'Dear Dr. Blackie,

'Believing it will not be without interest to you, I beg to send herewith a few photographs in connection with our trip to Killin. They are all taken by members of your party on the excursion day . . .

Yours obediently,
George Ritchie (Manager of
the Binding Department)'

The photographs taken by A. Baird, Press Revisor, Jos. Wright, Binder, Duncan Wright, Deaf and Dumb Binder, and others were contained in an album and served as a record of a happy outing.

We have seen how food played an important part in the success of any outing. The 'togetherness' engendered by a firm's outing did much to cement companionship when it came to drinking. The man who could down a substantial amount of beer gained in stature in the eyes of his fellow-workers. Drink was either carried on the coach, boat or train, or frequent stops were made so that parched throats could become unparched. The Temperance influence was also strong. It was, after all, the basis of Thomas Cook's business activities. Temperance Bands played at many of the outings, and certain occasions may have been 'dry'. Drink was cheap in the years before the Great War, but as can be seen from the accounts of outings already described in this chapter, strong drink was not splashed around, ginger beer, milk and tea being prominent beverages.

A spread of food was also essential. The working man's capacity to enjoy a variety of food was limited by his low wages. The sight of a sumptuous spread made mouths dribble with saliva in anticipation. The 'beano' that Robert Tressel describes in his book *The Ragged Trousered Philanthropists* took place annually (c. 1906) on the last Saturday in August. The men had been contributing to the cost—five shillings a head—for a month beforehand. On the day, instead of working until one o'clock, the men were paid an hour earlier and they hastily returned to their homes to change.

The brakes started from The Cricketers public house at one o'clock. There were four brakes altogether—three large for the men and one small one for the boss, Mr Ruston, and a few of his personal friends which included Mr Toonarf, an architect, and Mr Lettum, a house estate agent. One of the drivers brought a friend with a long coachman's horn. The friend was not paid for blowing it, but as he was out of work he could rely on a good meal, free drinks and possibly a collection for his efforts.

Before getting into the brakes, most of the men had had a drink or two and were smoking twopenny cigars. There was no jollity:

'To judge from the mournful expression on the long face of Misery, who sat on the box beside the driver of the first large brake, and the downcast appearance of the majority of the men, one might have thought it was a funeral rather than a pleasure party, or that they were a contingent of lost souls being conducted to the banks of the Styx. The man who from time to time sounded the coachman's horn might have passed as the angel sounding the last trump, and the fumes of the cigars were typical of the smoke of their torment, which ascendeth up for ever and ever.'

A brief stop was made at various picking-up points. Some of the men had taken their Sunday clothes out of pawn for the occasion; others had bought new suits paid for at a shilling a week. Half-hearted attempts were made at singing, but most of the party were hungry. They had had no time for a midday meal, but they wouldn't have eaten in any case as they wanted to save their appetites for the meal at The Queen Elizabeth which they reached at 3.40 p.m. The landlord announced that dinner would be served in ten minutes, but the party had already viewed the tables, covered with cloths,

'and the serviettes, arranged fanwise in the drinking glasses, were literally as white as snow, and about a dozen knives and forks and spoons were laid for each person. Down the centre of the tables glasses of delicious yellow custard and cut-glass dishes of glistening red and golden jelly alternated with vases of sweet smelling flowers.'

And the food:

'There was soup, several entrees, roast beef, boiled mutton, roast turkey, roast goose, ham, cabbage, peas, beans and sweets galore, plum pudding, custard, jelly, fruit tarts, bread and cheese and as much beer and lemonade as they liked to pay for, the drinks being an extra; and afterwards the waiters brought in cups of coffee for those who desired it.'

W. H. Smith's Warehouse (Printing Department) in Fetter Lane had an outing on 26 June 1909. The destination was the Ship Inn at Eastcote, near Pinner. Catching the 1 p.m. train from Marylebone they arrived at Pinner and strolled through some of the finest country in Middlesex to the Ship Inn at Eastcote where they were welcomed by their host, Mr Silvester. The extensive grounds of the Ship Inn were explored and after a splendid dinner the party adjourned to a cricket field and watched an exciting match, Married Men *v* Single Men. The Single Men won by three runs. Having survived the suspense of the match the party sat down to a tea which was all that could be desired. Then came the last event, a concert to which several members contributed, the star turn being a Mr Matts's rendering of 'She's My Daisy'. The health of the chairman having been drunk with musical honours, he proceeded to wind up the evening with a neat little speech entitled 'Our Department'. Having said 'au revoir' to the host, the party caught the 10.47 p.m. train back to London.

'My sisters (the Misses Colman), my husband and I are wishful to celebrate in some suitable way the 25th Anniversary of the foundation of the Carrow First Day School, with the start of which my father and mother were closely connected. We have decided that a suitable way to do this is to invite those members who are in regular attendance to spend a day in London as our guests . . . We have planned a route which will give those taking part in the expedition a bird's eye view of the chief historic spots of London. The expenses entailed by the train to and from London, entrance into the exhibitions, motoring round London and the meals will be defrayed by us. It has been a great pleasure to my husband, my sisters and myself to plan the expedition and we earnestly hope it may prove a pleasurable one to all who are able to take part in it.'

So wrote Mrs Stuart to Mr F. I. Beales, the superintendent of the Carrow Men's First Day School.* At 4.45 on Saturday, 11 June

* The Carrow Men's First Day School was founded in 1885. Besides un-

1910, a party of First Day Scholars ranging in age from seventeen to seventy left Norwich, each armed with a timetable giving particulars of places to be visited, meals, etc. and a specially compiled guide entitled 'A Day in London' in the form of a purple-covered booklet beautifully printed on art paper which had been carefully prepared by the Misses Colman.

The booklet contained a brief but comprehensive account of 'some events in the History of London' with descriptions of all the places of interest, monuments, pictures, art treasures, etc. The party arrived punctually at Liverpool Street Station at 7.20 a.m., where 'to the intense surprise and delight of the scholars', Mrs Stuart and the Misses Colman were waiting to receive their guests. Motor buses, in charge of Mr C. Stimpson, and conductors employed by Messrs Cook were boarded and the journey through London began. Those visiting London for the first time were heard to comment, 'Well, I *never*! Lawk a daisy! Mercy me!'

The timetable that the Misses Colman had so diligently prepared was as follows:

7.30 Start in Motor Busses for circular drive. The route leads past the Bank of England, the Mansion House, the GPO, on to Regent's Park, and past the entrance to the Zoo, then along Oxford Street and by the side of Hyde Park, past South Kensington Museum and eastwards past the National Gallery, the Courts of Justice, and St. Paul's Cathedral, through Cannon Street (108 Cannon Street is the London Office of J. & J. Colman Ltd.), crossing the Thames by London Bridge and back by the Tower Bridge.

10.   Reach the Tower of London.

10.45 Leave the Tower of London.

11.   Dinner at Slater's, 27 Leadenhall Street, E.C.

12.15 Drive westwards along the Thames Embankment visiting

12.45 The Houses of Parliament and Westminster Abbey.

1.45   Leave Westminster Abbey and drive to the Tate Picture Gallery

---

denominational religious instruction there was a Savings' Bank, Clothing Club, Sick Club, Coal Club, Self-Help Society and other useful facilities for the benefit of the employees of Messrs Colman. Two years later the Carrow Women's First Day School was formed.

2.35 Continue the drive westwards passing Buckingham Palace and the Albert Hall, arriving at

3.30 The Japan-British Exhibition at the White City. The party will be conducted through rooms 1 to 9 arriving

4. At the Machinery Hall Café for Tea.

6.30 Meet near the Wood Lane exit. The exact spot will be described when the party is at the Exhibition.

6.45 Start in busses for Liverpool Street Station.

8.15 Train leaves London. Supper served in train in two detachments.

10.45 Train due at Trowse.

10.50 Train due at Thorpe.

At the Japan-British Exhibition tea was served at one of Lyons' cafés and the party spent their time walking round the various exhibits, or by sitting quietly listening to the bands, or by riding on scenic railways and other ingenious contrivances of a surprising nature such as the flip-flap and wiggle-woggle.

Those not strong enough to stand the strain of so long a day were specially catered for. The supper in the train home was served on 'Daintily laid tables . . . abundantly supplied by the waiters with assiduous attention and marked politeness.' The carriages 'with electric lamps brilliantly lighted throughout' made a great impression. Another memento of the occasion was a packet of postcard views of the places visited, and each scholar received one.

The outing had gone without a hitch, and the next morning at full school 'opportunity was offered by the superintendent for the scholars to give expression to their feelings, when the prevailing note was one of thankfulness and gratitude'. And so ended an occasion which was given—to quote from the purple-covered booklet—

In Bright Memory of the Founders of the Carrow First-Day School, JEREMIAH JAMES COLMAN and CAROLINE COLMAN and of those Scholars of the School who have passed the Great Beyond:

> *'On the earth the broken arcs; in the heaven,*
> *a perfect round'*—R. Browning

On 22 June 1914 Huntley & Palmers organised a day outing for about 7,000 people and all the primary schools in Reading closed for the day so that the children could accompany their parents. From 3.30 a.m. until 6 a.m. the crowds arrived at the railway station to be greeted by music played by the Temperance Band. Ten special trains were waiting—five for Margate and Ramsgate with nearly 4,000 passengers, and five for Portsmouth with just over 3,000. Those who had selected the Kent resorts had continuous rain and thunderstorms from ten o'clock in the morning. Those who went to Portsmouth found the weather conditions ideal.

Almost a year before, on 4 July 1913, in order to celebrate the coming of age of Mr Geoffrey Colman, thousands of Carrovians who 'with sunshine in their breasts, together with a present of a day's wages, rail tickets and pin money in their pockets, sought with eager steps the yellow sands of Yarmouth, Lowestoft, Cromer, Sheringham and Mundsley', and one year later at the invitation of Mrs Stuart and the Misses Colman, who were responsible for the London outing already described, the women and girls employed at Carrow Works foregathered in the Carrow Gardens. At three o'clock the guests assembled and having been received in the Abbey by their hostesses 'proceeded to regale themselves with ices, under the stimulating influences of which they danced merrily on the lawn'.

The scene just described seems an appropriate one on which to bring down the curtain on an era. In just over one year there was to be an end to such charming occasions and when, some five years later, the curtain rose again, the scene had been changed. Attitudes were different, and the soulless grind of the Industrial Revolution had been replaced by better working conditions and a more—but not always much more—satisfactory worker-management relationship. At Huntley & Palmers, for example, a 48-hour working week was introduced and all workers received a week's holiday with pay. Consequently the old outings were automatically abolished.

When other firms resumed the annual outings there were differences. Familiar faces, old friends—they were no longer there. Outings now included women who, before the war, had been included as wives but not always as workers. The all-male and all-female outings which had been a tendency during the pre-war years were no longer applicable. Women, who had worked in factories and in offices helping in the war effort, were not prepared to settle for a life of domesticity at home. Holidays with pay meant that the outing was a pleasant bonus instead of, possibly, the 'holiday' it had been in the past. Although people still wore their Sunday best for outings, more casual costume was in evidence. The bowler hat, stiff collar, braces and waistcoat were discarded by the younger generation in favour of blazers, Oxford bags and 'co-respondent' shoes. Another important change was the popularity of the charabanc. It revolutionised the outing enabling those taking part to visit more out-of-the-way places which could not be reached by rail. The pattern of life had changed and the stability and peace of the Victorian and Edwardian periods were never to return.

4

'To Some Poor Child a Happy Day'

'In the hot and clouded alleys, round the stately Squares and Inns,
Where the brick and stone are scorching in the heat,
They are nursing withered flowers, they are playing with old tins,
They are picking up the matches in the street.
Won't you spare a single ninepence?
You will never feel the loss,
For it means to some poor child a happy day;
If it helps to ease one burden, if it aids to raise a cross,
Why you cannot call it money thrown away.'
                    J. A. Middleton, *Lady's Home Magazine*, c. 1904

In the grim lives that many children in Victorian and Edwardian
Britain were compelled to lead, there was at least one day in the
year that was remembered with pleasure—the annual outing.
Sunday Schools, charities or any society concerned with the welfare of children set aside a day in the summer to give children an
outing in the country or by the sea. Possibly it was the only holiday
the children had. The preparations were made and the outing paid
for in part or whole by charitably minded people who devoted
their spare time organising such events. State welfare barely
existed; the emphasis was on charity. The Lord of the Manor, or
perhaps his women-folk, were active. A day excursion for poor
children was achieved by the kindness of the well-to-do and the
Church who considered it their duty to look after those unfortunate youngsters whose very survival sometimes depended on the
benefits those with money and leisure chose to provide.

A merchant who worked from the Newcastle-upon-Tyne
Quayside, moved with compassion at the sight of the thousands of

poor children in the crowded city slums who rarely had an opportunity of breathing any pure air sent, in 1891, at his own expense, 120 of them to Monkseaton, where they had a day of real enjoyment. As a result, the Newcastle-upon-Tyne Poor Children's Holiday Association and Rescue Agency was formed, which in 1965 became the North East Children's Society with considerably wider powers to combat poverty amongst the young.

In 1893 clergymen, missionaries and other workers amongst the poor selected 3,000 children in Newcastle, and 100 in Gateshead and Felling Shore, all of any or no creed, and sent them to South Shields by the Tyne General Ferry Company's steamer in weekly batches of 250. On board were sandwiches, and at South Shields a substantial tea was supplied. Annually, thereafter, the Association aimed to 'provide a day's holiday at the seaside for every poor child in Newcastle who had no other means of enjoying one'.

In 1895, 7,617 children spent a full day's holiday at Tynemouth for £237 8s 10d, which paid for an enjoyable sail down the river and back, a substantial lunch on board the steamer and an abundant tea with fruit, consumed under cover by the sea shore.

The condition of the children who went on these outings were in many instances deplorable. Some of the boys were shoeless; others wore one boot. Some were bareheaded, and elbows and knees protruded from ragged clothing. The girls managed to look neater and tidier. A typical outing, in the latter part of the nineteenth century, is described by the Rev. Canon Franklin:

'Every Saturday during the summer season a steamer takes 300 poor children to the seaside ... At ten o'clock we embarked. Three hundred had marched through the city with the Chadwick Memorial Band at their head. The lanes and back streets, the fever dens and the underground dwellings, had given up their juvenile occupants, and like Falstaff's army they marched through the principal streets leading to the Quayside. Here the good steamship *Mabel* was ready. Soon all were comfortably seated, and the ladies and gentlemen who assisted Mr. Lunn, the chairman, and Mr. Watson, the secretary, were kindly solicitous for the happiness and ready to supply the wants of this army of waifs and strays, many of whom had never been on board before.

Screams of delight, varied by a running commentary of cheers, were kept up during the whole journey. The sons of toil, whether on shore or on board the ships we passed, responded to the cheers of the little ones . . . When we were half-way down the river . . . every child received a large meat sandwich, and soon there was silence on board. The mouth of the river was reached soon after eleven . . . The landing is soon effected and the band leads the way playing a joyful march towards the Aquarium. Here the little army is dispersed, and order gives way to a general rush for the sands; plodging and bathing and childish sports occupy them until three o'clock. A well-earned appetite draws our little friends around the tent before the hour, and every seat is occupied . . . I was requested to say a few words to the children; and then the largest buns I ever saw and mugs of tea were served to each, and for half-an-hour silence reigned while happiness beamed on the face of every one of those little ones. After satisfying their appetites many of them put aside a piece of cake for some absent one at home . . .'

On the return journey there were shouts of 'We're off to Canny Newcassel, we're off to Canny Newcassel, we're off to Canny Newcassel with a HIP, HIP, HIP, HURRAH!'

In 1887, in Glasgow, Walter Wilson of the Colosseum Warehouse, also moved by the plight of children in the city, treated 15,000 of them to an outing at Rothesay. Tickets were distributed by clergymen, missionaries and others who worked for the welfare of the poor, and five river boats and an ordinary steamer carried the party. Food was supplied on the journey and on arrival, consisting of 16,000 packages of buns, biscuits, scones and about 30 cases of oranges, 361 cases of sweets each containing about 640 packages, 8 cart-loads of milk and a similar amount of aerated water. The weather, although a little sultry, was otherwise excellent. Brass bands accompanied the excursionists and played on board and at arrival at Rothesay.

When the main body of the party had disembarked at Rothesay, the National Anthem was sung and there were speeches. Difficulties arose when it came to distributing the food 'as cakes and milk were somewhat slow in coming round, the children became impatient, and finally ignoring all orders, swarmed about the barricade from which the refreshments were being given out. Those who had received supplies and those who had not became indistinguishable, and, naturally the weak and the very young were the sufferers.'

There was, it seems, so much disorder that only part of the sports programme could be completed. Doubtless, however, the majority enjoyed themselves, and on their return to Broomielaw they were met by vast crowds of relatives and sight-seers.

In most of the accounts of these charity outings for children the unctuousness and patronising attitudes towards the poor by their 'betters' were evident. Above every other consideration, God granted all. It was due to His mercy, understanding and kindness, that the outing was taking place at all. The children were expected to say prayers and sing hymns, and to listen to dignitaries expound to them the glory of God. One can imagine the children fidgeting with impatience at being told how lucky they were when, not far away, the sea was lapping gently on to the sand, rocks were visible that cried out to be explored, or perhaps green grass in a field was waiting to be played on. It may have been a small price to pay for a day away from the squalor of normal surroundings.

Although the Victorian attitudes towards these children would find little favour in most quarters to-day, it must be appreciated that the absence of the welfare state placed the burden of lightening the lives of others on to the more affluent. There were wealthy people moved with genuine compassion at the plight of others, and they spent much time and money in trying to make life easier for those we would now refer to as the under-privileged. Within the context of the Victorian and Edwardian periods these attitudes are reflected in the words of the hymn 'All Things Bright and Beautiful':

> The rich man in his castle,
> The poor man at his gate,
> God made them, high or lowly,
> And order'd their estate.

The Fresh Air Fund was inaugurated in 1892 by Mr (later Sir) C. Arthur Pearson, publisher of *Pearson's Weekly* and other journals. The Fund worked in conjunction with the Ragged School Union, and by 1909 over two million children from London and cities in the provinces were taken from the slums to the

The G. Delgado staff outing to Margate, c. 1898, referred to in the
Introduction.

'To Brighton and Back for 3s 6d.' After the painting by Charles Rossiter.

Nineteenth-century music cover shows travelling conditions.

Entitled 'The Beach Hotel' this shows trippers on the sands, c. 1850.

Booking for an excursion train, 1872.

Waiting for the excursion train, 1880.

Trent Bridge excursion train disaster, 1869. 'The scene immediately after accident by our own artist on the spot.'

The beach at Hastings, 1857.

A day out in 1908 for the clerks at Cadbury's. On the left is the newly-built (1905) school, the gift of Mr George Cadbury.

MANCHESTER WORKING MAN *(who is going by the Sixpenny SUNDAY Excursion to Godley, Mottram, &c.)* :—
"Say, Mister, is this the Godley train ?"

STIGGINS :—" Godly train ! Alas my dear friend, I am constrained to say that it is NOT."

Sunday excursions were frowned upon. A nineteenth-century cartoon.

A day in the country for London children, 1872. Prayers with the provisions.

Prisoners in Mean Streets.

Tick off one square in a picture for every penny subscription. When you have all nine ticked, you have released one child from the prison bars of the slums for a day in the country.

SUBSCRIPTION FORM FOR PENNIES.

Two 'prisoners' released.

Employees of Laurence, Scott on a nineteenth-century river outing with musical accompaniment.

Bentalls' staff at Sunbury Lock in 1910.

The Independent Order of Good Templars Juvenile Spring Blossom
outing at Whitley Bay in 1898. The man kneeling on the sand is Mr
John King, a plumber for the Corporation. The girl kneeling on his left
(in her late eighties in 1975) was ten years old when the photo was taken.
Her father, standing at the back of the group, was an employee of Richard-
son's, a well-known local firm of decorators.

Staff outing to Sir George Chubb's home in Chislehurst, Kent, c. 1906.

Chelmsford Co-op staff outing, c. 1913.

The leather factory employees at Charles Letts off to Southend for the
day in 1912.

Pilkington's bevelling department set off for a day at Blackpool in the
1920s.

To the 1924 British Empire Exhibition at Wembley:
Boots of Nottingham by train.

Heelas of Reading by charabanc.

Bedminster Ebenezer Sisterhood outing, 27 June 1922.

Children's outing from Scunthorpe, 1925.

First Kodak
Staff Outing
~ Selsey ~
July 3rd 1927

K

Over 3,000 people attended the Times Publishing Company staff outing

country for a day's outing. In 1912 Millicent, Duchess of Sutherland explained that each ninepence subscribed by the public

'gives to one poor town child a day's holiday in the country—
a long day of purest happiness in green fields, forest glades, or by
the seaside, with romps and games, see-saws, and donkey rides,
cricket for the boys and kiss-in-the-ring for the girls, and fine
feasts for all on meat-pies and bread and butter and buns and
oranges—a day that is as a glimpse of Paradise to the poor little
mites who live in the darkness of squalid back courts and the
mean streets of our cities.'

As little as £8 2s paid the expenses of a party of 200 children
with attendants. In the journal *In His Name* of August 1892 this
hymn was printed, to be sung to the tune of Sir John Goss's Carol,
'See Amid the Winter Snow' (Novello & Co. Price 1d.):

HYMN FOR THE ANNUAL SUMMER OUTING
Now, Great God, to thee we pray
On our Summer holiday;
Go forth with us, and abide
All day long close by our side.
Once a year this day comes round;
Once a year this song shall sound;
Now be with us as we pray;
Grant us each a happier day.

The last verse:

Bring us safely back again,
Free from sorrow, harm and pain,
To the earthly home we love;
And, at last, to Heaven above.
Once a year this day comes round etc.

Crippled children excited pity and there is an account of small
groups of crippled children at Liverpool Station in 1895 making
their way laboriously along the platforms with their crutches and
high boots, while those too helpless even to walk were conveyed in
perambulators and bath chairs, their pale, marked faces of agony
making 'a touching picture in the busy life of our great city'. At

F

that time a deformed child—or adult for that matter—had only the crudest appliances to help them, and little was done to hide any disfigurement or to provide appropriate therapy that might enable them to lead more normal and useful lives. In 1898

'owing to the kindness of Mr. W. Copley Steane and other friends the [30] cripple children now staying at the Cripples Home at Bournemouth were taken to Swanage by steamer . . . On arriving at their destination the children were met by brakes and conveyed to Durlston Castle, where lunch and tea were provided. After lunch the party visited the caves and lighthouse. A short service was held on the cliffs, and the return steamer left at six o'clock. The cripples sang some of their sweet songs all the way home, and many passengers were touched by the pathetic sight.'

Some thirty years later, in 1927, five hundred Liverpool children assembled at Mersey Square, queued up for special tramcars at the depot and the first seven tramloads set out for Woodley. As the children crowded in, tightly hugging their coloured tickets for the outing, the boys of Offerton School, under Bandmaster Green, played 'Bam Bam Bammy Shore' and 'Bye, Bye, Blackbird' but, it is recorded, the children were too excited to join in the chorus. A far cry, indeed, from the hymns of the previous century.

The Demon Drink was an ever-present temptation to the older children—or so it was considered by officials of Dr Barnardo's in the 1880s. The following account is interesting because it draws attention to the danger. It was customary for Dr Barnardo's to send a number of children belonging to their Free Ragged Schools to the country for a day's 'pleasure', and in 1881 two trains from Burdett Road Station were booked and 2,500 children went for the day to Theydon Bois. The account of the outing is given in *Night and Day* of that year:

'A happier day some of the children, I am sure, never spent. Going by train we avoided that great temptation which conveyance by vans minister to—I mean the public house. When the omnibus vans are compelled to stop twice if not three times upon the journey to bait the horses, and the coachman too, it is not to be wondered at that, in a large excursion, having a number of vans, some of the older children should escape notice and enter the public house. I have long felt this to be a serious blot upon a "Day in the Country" scheme, and, realising the difficulties of the case, have not, since my eyes were opened to the danger, employed vans, nor am I likely ever again to do so.'

At Theydon Bois, within a few minutes the party was safe in a large field adjoining the forest, 'away from public houses and everything of that kind'. Nothing occurred to mar the day's enjoyment,

'and at half-past seven o'clock, having been well fed, pretty well tired, but thoroughly satisfied and happy, laden with ferns, grasses, wild flowers, branches ... the whole party re-formed and marched to the trains, reaching Limehouse again at about nine o'clock p.m., to be greeted by an immense concourse, which at one time must have numbered no fewer than eight or nine thousand people, three of the vast thoroughfares there being densely packed, far as the eye could reach. Every way from Burdett Road, over Victory Bridge, down Rhodeswell Road, and back again to St. Thomas's Road, all was a dense sea of spectators, assembled to welcome the children's return, and to behold the fireworks which friendly hands kindled, with a view to bring the day's proceedings to a close with *éclat*.'

The excursion cost 1s 2d a head which included the return journey, printing railway tickets, and a meal. The children brought with them bread and cheese, 'or fragments of other foods, to form an early dinner'.

The supervision of children and their welfare was a source of worry to officials and a formula for a successful children's outing was described by a writer in the Dr Barnardo's journal *Night and Day* of October 1883:

'1. Not to employ vans, which render stoppage at public houses absolutely necessary.
'2. To take care to have *separate* trains for the sexes, one for boys, one for girls, as also one for infants, so that however much overcrowding there may be, there can only be innocent fun, without temptations to indecorous behaviour.
'3. To bring no teachers or helpers who are not solemnly

pledged *to surrender themselves* to the well-being of the children *the whole day*, and to attempt no pleasuring on their own behalf, but to diligently watch over those of whom they start in charge. '4. To take great care that our destination is *as far removed from a public house as it is possible to be.*
'5. If we are compelled to pass a public house or to remain so near it as to create anxiety lest some of our older scholars should be drawn in, to *appoint a guard of our most prudent male* teachers to stand on duty near the entrance of the public house the whole time the party is near, and to challenge the entrance to it of any child or adult of our party.'

In the early 1860s the Sailors' Children's Society reported on this outing to their subscribers and friends:

'In August last the whole of *Children* had a trip to Scarborough, at the expense of your Treasurer. On arriving they were regaled with tea and spice cakes ... and by special invitation of Dr. Murray they assembled on the lawn opposite his house, where they sang several pieces. Twelve of the elder *Boys* were presented with a pocket knife, and twelve of the elder *Girls* with a pair of scissors, by the Venerable Doctor, who addressed them in a very touching manner, and was much affected by the sight of these dear orphan children. Several Ministers also, and other Gentlemen addressed the Children grouped on the *Sands* and a large and deeply affected company of Spectators made a collection of more than £6 for the Society. The sight of the *Children* at this fashionable watering place produced a strong feeling of sympathy in favour of your Society. . . .'

Every advantage was taken of this visit, for on the following Sunday the Rev. R. Balgarnie, 'the cordial friend of the Society', preached on the sands and made a collection towards the funds.

A worker at Dr Barnardo's took a keen interest in the branch of the East End Juvenile Mission known as 'The Union Jack Shoeblack Brigade' or 'Jack's Happy Home', which was situated on the edge of London's Limehouse Churchyard. In the worker's experience all boys and girls who attend a class or Sunday School 'considered themselves entitled to an excursion in the summer', and 'The Union Jacks' were no exception. These little urchins, scurrying about London's streets, picking up the odd penny or two as shoeblacks, were like Dickensian figures portrayed by Cruikshank, and the following description of the outings reflects the Victorian scene and attitude, and is therefore worth quoting at some length

'So it came about that one bright morning in August, eighteen of them, dressed in their smart sailor uniform, accompanied by their master and wife, met their teacher at Blackwell Pier, prepared to enjoy themselves. A pleasant day of it they had. Agreeable at all times, in fine weather, is a run down the river by steamer, and to the Limehouse shoeblacks, to whom such a treat was new, everything was full of interest—the big ships, the graceful yachts, the picturesque barges, and the views of Woolwich, Erith and other towns on its banks.

'Two ladies up from the country were of the party, and very novel to them was all they learnt as to the habits and customs of shoeblacks. They were surprised to find how well they live, and to hear from the matron of their odd tastes in eating, for the ladies could not have believed that the chief disadvantage of the boys' work is, that they can earn money too easily, though this is less the case, of course, with shoeblacks in the poorer parts of London.

'But nevertheless, it may readily be seen what an advantage it is to be able to put poor boys into a Home, where they can earn a livelihood at once, while something better is being found for them. The ladies are told of several former "Union Jacks", who are now doing well in other callings, where they could not have been placed direct from the streets, but to which the Home formed a stepping-stone. One of these had joined the party today—that respectable boy in a new grey suit, who has managed to obtain a holiday, and took the opportunity of spending it with his old Brigade.

'Arrived at their destination, Rosherville Gardens, the boys first have lunch, and then disperse to see the wonderful sights and roam about the pretty grounds till tea-time. This meal is held in the Swiss Cottage, where shrimps and cake, as much as the boys can eat, make it a substantial bill of fare, and afterwards, by way of grace, they sing one of their hymns. Sweet voices have several of the lads, and the hard-worked maid-servants at Rosherville Gardens stop to listen as they sing—

> I shall never be confounded,
> I am trusting in that word,
> I am trusting, fully trusting,
> Sweetly trusting in His word.

'Then, in the grounds, the boys with their master and teacher, get out a rope, and play "the tug of war", a game learnt at Wimbledon Camp, where the Brigade goes, once a year, to pick up waste paper. But the day is drawing to a close, and there is still the return journey to be performed; so presently a scamper is made for the boat, and whiling the way with songs, they steam up to London, all agreeing that they have had a delightful excursion . . .'

One can sympathise with these boys having to wear sailor suits on such an occasion and being subject to military discipline and the patronising attention of the ladies in the party. The inference that it was possible for them to earn too much money in the more prosperous areas of London comes strangely from those whose wealth was acquired less haphazardly. It is possible to visualise the group of cheeky, alert little cockneys singing hymns in their 'sweet voices', their smart sailor suits surely somewhat crumpled at that stage of the day. Despite the restrictions which to-day would be unacceptable, that day outing constituted a 'holiday' which was doubtless welcome under almost any circumstances. The final touch must surely be the reference to the 'tug of war' game which was learnt at a camp where the boys went annually, not necessarily to enjoy themselves, but to pick up waste paper carelessly discarded by their elders and betters.

Picnics were a popular form of outing in the 1880s. Dr Barnardo's would bring together six, eight or ten families, and at two o'clock in the afternoon the farm cart arrived to receive the tea things—urns of tea, and the boxes, baskets and bundles of bread-and-butter, cake, mugs. When all this was loaded the little girls from three years of age upwards would fill the cart to capacity, and the old grey mare would jog along at a quiet, contented pace until Epping Forest was reached. Following close behind would be a party of walkers. At seven in the evening the journey homeward began. Picnics in West Ham Park involved a walk to Ilford of 2½ miles, a railway journey to Forest Gate of ten minutes, and a walk of fifteen minutes to the park gates, and the same on the return journey. 'But this by no means is too much for a large number of our girls, who were glad of the opportunity for so long a stretch', states a report which continues, 'Thus the weeks pass gaily away without any accident, or any serious ailment, or any disaster, through the watchful goodness of our gracious God.'

The outings for poor children relied on money from public and no effort was spared to enlist the sympathy of those who could afford to give. Dr Barnardo's journal *Night and Day* of 1879 appealed on these lines, 'I am anxious to take some 2,300 children of our Free Day and Sunday Schools for a day in the country. The expense of conveyances, food etc. for the day is only 1s 4d per child, or £1 6s 8d for every twenty children. May I appeal to my readers to place this desirable boon before every child in our Ragged Schools?'

In the same journal a year later, a correspondent points out that on the way home from a day's excursion in the country with a number of poor children, they passed an imposing building—a Home for Lost Dogs. It drew comments from the assembled company and one of the youngsters remarked, 'Just think o' that ... Why, if it ain't a home for pups! Think o' people givin' a grand place like that for lost dawgs. I expect they have a fine time of it inside and plenty o' grub.' The correspondent points out that there are many who will give to animal welfare but few who will contribute money to reclaim human waifs and strays.

As the horse brakes drew up outside the fine houses in London's squares during August, the servants assembled in the doorway to supervise the loading of the many items of luggage, and to bid farewell to the master, mistress and children on the way to the seaside. When they had gone, there was much to do to make the house habitable for the return of the family a month or more later. Watching the annual exodus were what *Punch* likes to call 'their less fortunate neighbours', consisting of urchin children, mothers carrying babies, old men in rags, bent double. As the brake drove off down the street, those fortunate enough to be inside would have seen their less fortunate neighbours' disperse to their impoverished homes. Did they wonder what the long, hot, summer days held in store for such people? Possibly, but there was little that could be done about what was a fact of life. It may have satisfied them to know that the children and perhaps their mothers would get a holiday after all. A day in the country or by the sea was referred to as a 'holiday'. So it was all right. Everybody had a holiday.

At least the ragged street musician followed his wealthy patrons to the seaside resorts. *Punch* in 1872 shows a housemaid outside a smart town house handing a crippled, threadbare musician a coin. From the window of the house a group of well-fed, bright-eyed children watch the scene. The housemaid explains to the musician that he need not call again as they are all going to the seaside on Saturday. 'Tell the Lady I'm much obliged,' says the musician eagerly taking the coin, 'and I'm going to the seaside myself next week!'

In the 1840s the Temperance Excursion Committee issued an address to the clergy, gentry, tradesmen and other benevolent people in Preston, Lancashire, and the vicinity, stating that arrangements had been made for treating the poor and needy, the aged and infirm, with a gratuitous trip to Fleetwood. Every benefactor making a donation of £1 was entitled to forty tickets which would be distributed only to the poor. Those who objected to having to do the distributing could seek help from the Committee which considered that, as railway trips were available to all classes, it was very desirable that the poorest classes should not be overlooked.

Every effort was made to see that the poorest had a 'holiday'. In 1907 Marie Corelli wrote a poem for the benefit of the Fresh Air Fund. Here is the first verse:

> Pity the children of the poor,
> Who've never plucked the daisies,
> Who've never watched the skylark soar,
> Or heard it singing praises:
> Who've never trod the fresh green sward,
> Or rambled by the river;
> They need a holiday, ye rich—
> May God reward the giver.

In the late 1920s and early 1930s a Committee known as the Poor Children's Outing Fund, supported by business firms and local Workmen's Social Clubs, organised a day out to Whitley Bay for poor children in the Stanley and Consett area of Durham. Active support was also given by the employees of the Stanley coach and bus garage who at that time ran a concert party known as the Northern Lights.

In those depressed years the outing was a happy occasion for the children, most of whom never saw the sea from one year to the next. A convoy of as many as 125 buses filled with children (each provided with a bag of buns and a small amount of spending money) left Stanley for Whitley Bay at nine o'clock on a week-day morning. At seven o'clock the return journey began, and this huge convoy, passing through the villages, would bring the inhabitants from their houses to wave and cheer the tired but happy children on the way home.

5

Nearly all at Sea

'I'm on the Sea!
I'm where I didn't ought to be,
For first I'm above, and then I'm below,
Oh! Captain it's dreadful to serve me so.'
From the song *The Excursion Train*
written by W. F. Vandervell, c. 1870

The rush to the sea in the nineteenth century not only gave the hard-working population from the towns and cities an opportunity to inhale health-giving ozone, but people were eager to bathe in it and even travel on it. An excursion by steamer had much to commend it. There was more opportunity for 'togetherness' than in a train, where everybody was confined to compartments in which there was little room to move about; the novelty of eating and drinking on board was appealing and the fact that the steamer had left England's shores was exciting. On board there was space for entertainment, bands and dancing. River and canal excursions, although lacking the excitement of the open sea, enabled those taking part to see aspects of the countryside hitherto hidden from them.

The success of a steamer outing depended on good weather. The day might begin fine but by the end of the day storm clouds could gather which would dampen the high spirits of those on board and compel some to expel into the sea the food and drink they had indulged in earlier. The vessel could become a living hell with no means of escape until she docked, when the unfortunate excursionists staggered about on dry land and made for home as quickly as possible.

Perhaps one of the most delightful descriptions of a sea excursion is by Charles Dickens in *Sketches by Boz*, in which the reader is introduced to Percy Noakes, a law student living in chambers on the 4th floor at Gray's Inn Square. He was 'a devilish good fellow' who decided to take a party on a sea excursion down to the Nore and back and have a splendid cold dinner laid out in the cabin before starting, and lunch laid out on deck. A steamer was hired for the party. A band would play so that those taking part could dance the quadrille all day on an appropriately chalk-marked deck. Anybody with any musical talent was invited to make himself (or herself) useful. There was Mr Hardy, a stout gentleman of about forty, who had a reputation—thoroughly deserved as it turned out—of being the life and soul of the party. 'He could sing comic songs, imitate hackney-coachmen and fowls, play airs on his chin, and execute concertos on the Jew's-harp . . . He had a red face, a somewhat husky voice, and a tremendous laugh.'

The eventful day arrived. Every member of the committee was instructed to wear a piece of blue sarsenet ribbon round his left arm. The boat—the *Endeavour*—belonged to the General Steam Navigation Company and was lying off the Custom House. Dinner and wines were provided by 'an eminent purveyor'.

Noakes clambered on board at 7 a.m. to supervise the arrangements. This was well in advance of the Committee and company generally who were not due for another two hours. Mr Hardy—a prominent Committee member—was dressed 'in a blue jacket and waistcoat, white trousers, silk stockings, and pumps—in full aquatic costume, with a straw hat on his head, and an immense telescope under his arm'. The rest of the Committee dressed in 'white hats, light jackets, waistcoats and trousers' looking like something 'between waiters and West Indian planters'.

Then the company arrived with three guitars and an immense portfolio of music. Although the boat was ready to go, more passengers were sighted, consisting of parents and children, a girl of about six and a boy of four. The girl was dressed in a white frock, with a pink sash and a 'dog's-eared-looking little spencer; a straw bonnet and green veil, six inches by three-and-a-half'. The boy was in a nankeen frock 'between the bottom of which, and the top of his plaid socks, a considerable portion of two small mottled legs were discernible'. He wore a light blue cap with a gold band and tassel. In his hand he held a 'damp piece of gingerbread . . . with which he had slightly embossed his countenance'.

The boat got under way at last and the band played 'Off she
goes'. Sailing briskly down the Pool, past the Docks and the
Thames Police Office, the young ladies exhibited 'a proper display
of horror at the appearance of the coal-whippers and ballast-
heavers'.

Hardy told stories to the married ladies at which they laughed
very much into their pocket-handkerchiefs, and hit him on the

BRIERDEAN BRIDGE
TO BE OPENED
On THURSDAY, 18th June,
BY A
PUBLIC
DEJEUNER.

The Committee beg to acquaint Ladies and Gentlemen desirous of being
present, that every arrangement is made for their comfort. The Tent will be elegantly
Fitted-up and Decorated for the occasion, with a Double Covering to prevent damp-
ness. A BAND OF MUSIC is engaged; and the Committee have also pleasure in
saying they have entered into agreement with the Proprietors of that Large and
Powerful New Steam Packet

The Prince Albert,

Which Vessel will leave the NEW QUAY, NORTH SHIELDS, Precisely at ONE o'Clock, with the BAND, and will proceed as far as SEATON
SLUICE, (Wind and Weather Permitting), to take in those Ladies and Gentlemen belonging that Neighbourhood.
N.B. The Boat being at the Sole Expense of the Committee, none but Persons with Tickets for the Dejeuner, and their Friends, will be admitted
on Board.
Culvert Inn, Brierdean Bridge, 13th June, 1840.

PRINTED AT THE PORT OF TYNE PILOT OFFICE, NORTH SHIELDS.

knuckles with their fans, declaring him to be 'a naughty man—a
shocking creature'. Quadrilles were danced, Hardy playing
'brilliant fantasies on the Jew's-harp'. Duets were sung and there
was a Spanish composition for three voices and three guitars.

The cry 'Dinner's on the table, ladies' heralded a change in the
weather. The sky became more and more overcast. From 'spitting'
with rain it became a steady downpour. The boat rocked. 'There
was a large, substantial, cold boiled leg of mutton at the bottom of
the table, shaking like a blancmange; a previously hearty sirloin of
beef looked as if it had been suddenly seized with the palsy; and

some tongues, which were placed on dishes rather too large for them, went through the most surprising evolutions; darting from side to side, and from end to end like a fly in an inverted wine-glass . . .' There were demands for small glasses of brandy. Seats seemed to slide away from those seated, and by the time the cloth was removed for dessert the company staggered on deck, the ladies muffled in shawls. The *Endeavour* arrived at the Custom House at two o'clock the following morning, the passengers in a poor way, but Percy Noakes was 'as light-hearted and careless as ever'.

In July 1839 a novel and interesting excursion was announced 'by that favorite [sic] steam packet *Comet* to Rochester Bridge'. G. Gore, steward of the *Comet*, 'begs respectfully to inform his Friends and the Public, that he has engaged the above celebrated Packet for an Aquatic Trip'. The vessel left London Bridge Wharf at 8 a.m., calling at the Royal Terrace Pier, Gravesend, from there Round the Nore, and up the Medway, calling at Sheerness. Passengers wishing to land there could be picked up on the return journey from Rochester Bridge where they were given two hours ashore to visit Her Majesty's Fleet and 'the splendid ruins of the old Castle'. Military and Quadrille Bands were in attendance and the dancing was conducted by 'Professional Gentlemen'. Provisions and wines were of the best quality and the fare from London was 5s. Tickets were on sale mostly at taverns in the riverside parishes.

A year earlier, in 1838, excursionists to Greenhithe, Northfleet and Gravesend were invited to board one of the numerous steam packets sailing every morning from St Katherine's and London Bridge Wharves, and to admire 'the ingenuity of man' in the adoption of steam for maritime purposes. Who would have believed a few years previously that steam-vessels would be just as certain and regular as the stage coach? Passengers boarding the former found the accommodation so convenient, the cabins being 'fitted up in the most splendid style, and with every possible attention to comfort'.

An early pleasure excursion in Bournemouth in 1886 was arranged for the occasion of the Shah of Persia's visit to Britain. A Mr David Sydenham chartered a steamer from Southampton, the *Fawn*, for a trip to Spithead where a review was to be held in the visitor's honour. Eventually a company was formed under Sydenham's management, but it was not financially rewarding. In 1871 Mr George Burr of Swanage purchased the *Heather Bell*, a Clyde-built steamer with a carrying capacity of 246 and capable of travelling at nine miles an hour. It had 'spacious saloons fitted up with every regard to comfort', and the Bournemouth Promenade Band generally accompanied the *Heather Bell* on her excursions. Although everything was done to make the service popular, Burr announced his wish to retire and withdrew the steamer from service. In 1879 there were two companies running excursions and competition was so keen that the excursionist could go to the Isle of Wight and back for 4½d. In those competitive days one boat, the *Transit*, had the Royal Italian Band aboard playing selections from popular operas, while the competing ship, the *Royal Saxon* boasted Messrs Roberts and Archer's Dramatic Company, although the bills announcing the excursion did not reveal what was being performed.

In 1890 the Rev. Alfred Binnie reported to his parishioners in the St Nicholas Parish Magazine as follows:

'The Vicarage, Kenilworth,
July, 1890

'Dear Friends,
'Since I last wrote we have been abroad to Portsmouth and the Isle of Wight. The morning was not very promising and some thought we were going to have a wet day. Nevertheless the train started punctually at 5 a.m. with a good company, amid cheers from not a few on the platform, who came to bid us farewell. Passing Leamington on the Great Western line we went via Oxford, Basingstoke and Winchester to Portsmouth, arriving there at ten minutes past nine.

'The first building that attracts your notice on leaving the station is the New Town Hall, which certainly will be a very handsome one when it is finished.

'Some went straight to *The Victory* and saw the place where the great Nelson died, fighting for his country.

'Then we paid a visit to the Dockyards, where they were very busy, and we learnt that Kenilworth supplies a brave sailor who was on board one of the best men-of-war ships, *The Howe*, was preparing to sail in a few days. We visited the *Serapis*, a troop ship, which can carry 2,000 men, only there cannot be much room to spare. Also we went on board the *Hecla*, and one of the Chief Officers explained the manner of working the torpedoes.

'The Isle of Wight was a source of great attraction, the sea was very calm and we only wished the passage had been longer.

'Some went into the interior of the Island, some enjoyed the Promenade at Ryde, others took a dip into the sea. The Electric Railway on the Pier was well patronised.

'In the evening we finished up with a drive round Southsea.

'Punctually at 8 we started homewards, and arrived at Kenilworth about 12.30. At the station we sang the Doxology and returned to our homes, after spending a very happy day, full of thankfulness that we were home in safety and that no one was left behind.

'I must confess that I have always noticed on these trip days that everybody seems to be determined to enjoy the day in a rational way, and to help others to be happy, and I think we feel more like one family than at any other time. 258 adult tickets, 98 children's tickets and 8 extension tickets were sold, making a total of 364.'

I am indebted to Mr T. R. Fancott of Kenilworth for the above who writes: 'My father once told me that when the parish outing arrived at their destination a telegram was despatched to the Kenilworth Post Office notifying their safe arrival. This telegram was then displayed in the Post Office window to inform those who stayed behind that the outing had safely reached their destination.'

On 27 September 1841 a combined sea and rail excursion was organised. A special twenty-carriage train left Nine Elms at 6.45 a.m. with over 300 passengers, a further 100 joining at Woking. The party arrived at Southampton at 9 a.m., embarking on the *Grand Turk* to sail round the Isle of Wight returning to Southampton via Spithead at 5 p.m. The train left Southampton at 6 p.m. and the distance covered was 220 miles by land and sea for £1. A remarkable achievement at that time.

Boating expeditions, so pleasant in prospect, were not always so enjoyable in reality. Stead, McAlpine & Co. Ltd, calico printers of Cummersdale near Carlisle went to Silloth on 2 August 1873. The boring speeches out of the way, a member of the firm wrote these verses ('expressly for fun') to describe the scenes that followed:

Now full of cakes and mischief, they all made for the boat;
Never before was such a cargo of *cherubs* sent afloat
Their chief he gaily paced the deck, and proudly on them smiled,
To use a common simile, like father on his child.
The *cherubs* were gaily singing, when the vessel left the pier
But as we met the flowing tide they soon felt rather queer.
The boat began to pitch a bit, t'was sailing against the breeze,
The chief thus squaring his account, might well suggest a wreck.
Soon half-digested buns and milk was flooding all the deck
Mixed up with a few *cherubs* who had implored in vain
The Captain for to turn back, and take them home again
To save them from suffocation in their own milky tide . . .

Huddled on deck the passengers slept away their fear, and the verse continues:

And all were alive and kicking, soon as we reached the pier
Well blown about and weary, each gladly sought the train
Not sorry that the day was done and start for home again.

In about 1860, R. Thorpe & Co., colliery owners, took their workmen and boys of the Honey Well, Willow Bank and North Gawber Collieries on an outing to Hull from North Gawber, near Barnsley. At Goole they boarded the *Princess*, *Colin Campbell* and *Vine* and sailed down the Ouse to Hull, where they disembarked and toured the town. On the way back, down came the rain. A member of the party on the *Princess* relates how the vessel, on leaving Hull in a gale and rain, was subjected to so much tossing and heaving that the pumps had to be used. Water was scattered all over the excursionists and many hats were wafted overboard, never to be found again.

Poor Billy Scholey, one among the rest,
Thus lost his *tile*—he said it was his best,
But then the scholars of that motley school
Bought him another when he got to Goole.

An additional compensation was that the sun shone again.

That keen excursionist, the Rev. Francis Kilvert, so energetic on land was equally purposeful at sea, and his description of a steamship outing shows what he and his companion had to endure. Despite forebodings from the Testament ('There came down a great storm of wind upon the lake and the ship was filled with violence of the waves'), the Rev. Francis Kilvert took his mother on a voyage in a steamboat from Weston-super-Mare to Ilfracombe, some fifty-four miles down the Channel. It was 10 September 1852. The steamboat arrived at the Weston Pier at 9.15—an hour late. There was a slight swell as the passengers were embarking. Those on board who were in their 'best dresses and ribbons, laughing and talking, joking and prepared to enjoy the voyage became gradually grave, serious, silent, melancholy, white, yellow and green, and one by one retired to the gunwale and kneeling up on the bench hung their heads dismally and hopelessly over the side. They looked as if they were engaged in private prayer or in some sort of worship to the sea.'

All this, however, had no effect on the reverend gentleman and his mother, who both remained disgustingly healthy. Out in the Channel the swell increased and, running as they were against the tide and wind, the boat started pitching and tossing and shipping water. The sailors had forgotten to open the scuppers and the salt water was surging around the deck up to the passengers' ankles. Mother put her feet up on the bench and held on to the ropes for dear life. Others, less robust, were too wretched to care about anything and sat with their feet and ankles in the water. Some had lost all care of their appearances, their clothes pulled back over their knees. Mother, except for the water, was perfectly content and 'greatly enjoyed the motion of the vessel'. The Rev. Kilvert much preferred the quick pitching and tossing of the boat to the long, slow heave which, in the descent, brought his stomach fairly into his mouth.

These two must have been the only passengers to admire the beautiful views along the Somerset and North Devon coasts—the bright red cliffs and brilliant green of the meadows. The steamboat dropped anchor at Ilfracombe at 3 p.m.—two hours late. It had taken five hours to travel the fifty-four miles. The captain shouted that he was only staying an hour, so it seemed hardly worth while going ashore. As there was no pier the passengers had to be landed in open boats, 'the ladies being lifted in a scrambling way down off the deck into the boats by the sailors, putting their

G

arms round the sailors' necks'. This did not suit mother or her son, who remained on deck from where they could see at the foot of a huge grey cliff some tiny bathing machines. Men were bathing and plunging from a spring diving board in full view of the boat and 'one man swam round our vessel looking all the world like a frog as he swam naked close beneath the stern in the clear blue water'.

It was a long, weary voyage back. Another five hours of discomfort until some must have wondered if they would ever get home. But Kilvert and his mother found much to enjoy. 'It was pretty to watch all the different lights along the coasts. The flat Holme light, the Burnham light, the revolving or intermittent flashes from the *Breaksea* lightship on the Culver sands and the further one in Clevedon Bay.' Every light on Cardiff pier and along the docks could be seen. 'The whole sea was lighted around us and the Channel seemed alive with lights.'

It had been a punishing excursion but least two passengers had weathered the storm and found much to enjoy.

Further afield, in Scotland, the Clyde steamers were sailing from Glasgow to the lochs carrying passengers in their thousands, who longed to get away from the confining conditions under which they lived. It is a romantic story told by Alan J. S. Paterson in his book *The Victorian Summer of the Clyde Steamers (1864– 1888).**

A Grand Pleasure Excursion to Loch Long and Loch Lomond was announced for 14 August 1878 on the saloon steamer *Bonnie Doon*, sailing from Ayr to Arrocher, Troon and Ardrossan in the early morning and arriving at its destination about 12.30 p.m. 'The scenery of this Route opens up the Gems of the far-famed Firth of Clyde, the Mountain ranges of Arran, the Verdant Island of Bute, the wooded shores of Cowal, and the magnificent Alpine Scenery of Loch Long; Loch Lomond, "the Queen of the Scottish Lakes", surrounded with its majestic and precipitous mountains, and studded over with its green islands reposing in fairy loveliness, all combine to form a scene of grandeur and variety which cannot be surpassed.' Such lyrical descriptions could not be resisted, but if money was the trouble 'To Garelochhead for 2d' headed the announcement of cheap trips in the *Loch Foyle*. For

* David & Charles

that sum one travelled steerage, but if another threepence could be raised it was possible to travel cabin class.

The steamer *Hero* sailed to Lochgoilhead and 'Capt. McPherson', it was stated, 'has kindly consented to exhibit his Patent Boat-lowering Apparatus during the Trip. Passengers will thus have an opportunity of judging its efficiency for saving life at sea.' Other excursions were announced for the *Hero* and the *Vivid* to Partick, Renfrew, Bowling, Dumbarton, Greenock, Gourock, Dunoon and Largs, when it was stated 'there will be a grand Musical Promenade on Dumbarton Pier at which the Dumbartonshire Battalion Band will be in attendance, and play selections of their choicest Music. There will also be several Races and other Land Sports.'

In 1870 the Carters Association excursion, which was an annual event, consisted of a party of 800. They embarked on the *Rothesay Castle* for Lochgoilhead. The excursionists marched to Broomielaw in the early morning and back into the city on their return in the evening. It is small wonder that the streets were packed with people, especially in the evening. Each way they formed a procession headed by a Rifle Volunteer Band riding a large waggon drawn by eight horses, while bringing up the rear were the office-bearers of the Association, each wearing a bright-coloured sash and a broad Kilmarnock bonnet. All were mounted on horseback.

The crowds must have been offensive to more sensitive souls because in 1882 an announcement highlighting comfort and exclusiveness on board the *Ivanhoe* specified in no uncertain way that 'as this STEAMER DOES NOT SAIL TO OR FROM GLASGOW, PASSENGERS may rely on having a PLEASANT SAIL without the Ordinary Rabble common on Board Clyde Steamers during the Glasgow Fair', which was holiday time for the city's workers.

A feature of a day excursion arranged by the Glasgow and Inverary Steamboat Company was to take passengers to watch massive rock blasts at the Crarae quarries on the western shores of Loch Fyne, after which the steamer—*Lord of the Isles*—continued to Inverary. In September 1886 it was announced that 'ANOTHER MONSTER BLAST (7 Tons Gunpowder)' had been arranged so that the explosion took place on the arrival of the *Lord of the Isles* opposite the quarries, when the ship would signal for the spectacle to take place. The announcement added, 'It has also been arranged for those desirous of inspecting the Quarry after the Blast, that they may be landed at Crarae Pier and taken up again on the return of the steamer from Inverary.'

On that particular 25 September it was a dull, overcast day and on board were a number of Glasgow Councillors. A blast from the ship's siren was the signal for the gunpowder to be ignited and the explosion that followed was impressive. Three hundred passengers—mainly men and children—landed at the quarries to inspect the result of the explosion as advertised. The ladies, for the most part, due to the inclement weather and lack of interest, preferred to remain on board and proceed to Inverary.

When those who had disembarked arrived at the quarry, they went inside to view the mass of stone which had been displaced. Suddenly, a boy staggered and fell and later others, overcome by poisonous fumes, also collapsed to the ground. It was a horrifying spectacle that confronted the passengers of the *Lord of the Isles* as the ship returned from Inverary. The corpses were loaded on to the ship as well as those affected by the fumes, and it was a melancholy journey back to Glasgow, where the news had been received. Large crowds gathered on the quayside to watch the dead and injured taken off.

Something must have gone very wrong on the *Rothesay Castle* on the occasion of the Coatbridge Phoenix Iron Works excursion in August 1865. An advertisement inserted in the *Glasgow Herald* on 4 August stated:

COATBRIDGE PHOENIX WORKS EXCURSION
'The annual excursion of the above works took place yesterday in the splendid new steamer *Rothesay Castle* to Rothesay, where they spent a very harmonious and agreeable day. The band, under the leadership of Mr. John Lindsay, Coatbridge, discoursed most excellent music on the way down, and enlivened the field during the sports with appropriate airs, and the whole excursionists enjoyed themselves as merry as a marriage bell, until, on their return journey, they were highly dissatisfied with the treatment they received from the agents and captain of the splendid new steamer *Rothesay Castle* and treated them on disembarkation with three hearty groans.'

What caused the groans is not known.

The river was also popular. Many firms took their employees on the Thames, including Huntley & Palmer whose first 'aquatic excursion' took place in 1855, when about 200 employees, wives, children and 'female friends' visited Park Place near Henley. It was repeated the following year when one of the pleasure boats was dressed overall with the flags of the Crimean allies. In the summers of 1857 and 1858 river trips were made to Coombe Lodge, between Pangbourne and Basildon.

Three pleasure boats were hired—*Queen of the Thames, Prince of Wales* and *Princess Royal*. Captain Codd and his band of the Royal Berkshire Militia, together with a Quadrille band, were in attendance, and on arrival in the grounds archery contests and cricket matches took place while the youngsters—the average age was low—played boisterous games like 'He' and danced the time away. After tea George Palmer with his friends joined the party. On the return journey to Reading, the bands, encouraged only with non-alcoholic beverages, accompanied the singing collectively and solo. The noise from the pleasure boats carried far into the night and at each riverside village groups of people assembled to wave the excursionists on their way. Reading reached, the National Anthem was sung before everyone dispersed for home.

In June 1909 the Counting House of W. H. Smith & Son Ltd proposed an outing on a launch *My Queen* from Cookham to Windsor and back. The anticipation so inspired a participant that he contributed this verse to *The Newsbasket*, the company's house journal:

MY QUEEN
(Dedicated to the Officers of the Counting House Outing)

When and how shall I earliest board her?
On the ocean or up the stream?
I hope the Committee can well afford her,
For they say as a launch she's quite a dream.
'With the self-same sunlight streaming upon her'
That comes in the song—you know what I mean—
She is somewhere moored and soon I'll be on her,
The launch that I waited for, 'My Queen! My Queen!'

Sadly, when it came to the day, the party set sail in a launch named the *Balmoral*!

Miss Molly Pardoe of Malvern describes a trip on a canal that took place in about 1911:

'When I was a child, a Mr. Hughes, Boat Builder of Selly Oak, Birmingham, would hold back his last two boats from sale— open boats which would ultimately be used as coal barges— until after the Annual Outing of the Sunday School, of which he was President. It was amazing to see how the Sunday School grew in size a few weeks prior to the Outing.

'The barges, filled with children, all in their best clothes, accompanied by Sunday School teachers, were towed by horses along the canal past Barnt Green, which entailed going through a long dark, black oozing tunnel. We were advised to take waterproofs (insufficient space for brollies) to protect us through the tunnel from the incessant drip, drip of the black slime off the roof of the tunnel, and to keep our fingers away from the edge of the boat because our fingers could be badly crushed between the barge and the walls of the tunnel. It was a tight fit.

'To this day—sixty-three years later—I can vividly recollect the feeling of cold desolation, and quiet awe, as we watched the patch of daylight gradually receding and decreasing until it was a tiny white spot, and then total blackness. The only sound was the lapping of the water against the tunnel walls, and the occasional mutter of the bargees as they manœuvred the barge through the tunnel by stout poles, and I seem to remember (with horror) that they also used their hands on those slimy walls and roof to propel the barge along.

'At long last, or so it seemed, because remember progress was very slow, the quiet would be broken by a cry, "There it is", and our spirits rose as we saw ahead a tiny spot of light which slowly increased in size until we were out into the daylight, to tea and games in a field.'

Another recollection is of a canal trip from near Darlington Wharf in a transformed coal barge. A member of the party, dressed in spotless white flannels wishing to move, found that he had stuck to the tarry side of the barge.

There is a story supplied by Mrs Lymen of Moseley, Birmingham, who recollects it being told by the Minister of her Church.

The story concerns sixteen elderly ladies of Mablethorpe, Lin-colnshire, who in about 1913 planned to go on an outing to a nearby island. It was a beautiful morning as they boarded the ferryboat, and as soon as it got under way the ladies crowded to one side of the boat to wave to their friends who had come to see them off. In spite of warnings, the boat heeled gently over, depositing the ladies equally gently into the water, which was not so deep to prevent them scrambling ashore. But the day was spent in bed in the Infirmary while their clothes dried out.

The P.L.A. Monthly of February 1932 announced the launching in time for Whitsun of that year of 'the most luxurious and up-to-date pleasure steamer ever built specially for Londoners'. Capable of carrying over 2,000 passengers, it boasted a glass-covered lounge 130 feet long on deck, four private dining rooms each designed to accommodate a dozen people, while in the main dining saloon 300 could be served at a sitting. She was built by Cammell Laird for the General Steam Navigation Company's London to Southend, Margate and Ramsgate service. Cooking on such vessels at that time was done on coke stoves independent of the general fuel system, but in this unnamed paddle-boat oil was to be used for cooking for the first time.

On 23 August 1934 the *Royal Eagle* left Tower Pier at 11 p.m. for a Harvest Moon all-night Gala Cruise. The hours were spent either dancing and watching 'entertainment by professional jesters' or consuming supper and breakfast. Sunrise revealed the sea, but the ship was back at Tower Pier at seven o'clock the following morning. Considerable efforts were made to keep the passengers happy at all times. To 'trip it on the light fantastic toe' was made easy on the spacious deck. Drafts, chess boards and other games were provided and refreshments 'of the best quality' were available on board at moderate charges. Directly the ship sailed an excellent plain breakfast for 1s could be eaten, and ham, eggs, etc. were in abundance at a trifling charge.

Nevertheless as early as 1929 steamboat pleasure traffic on the Thames between London and the East Coast resorts was not believed to be a paying proposition. Even a fine, hot summer failed to bring an adequate return to the owners. The season was short, most of the traffic was confined to week-ends, and for the greater part of the year the vessels were laid up. There were too many steamers and the takings were beginning to show that there was competition from traffic on the road.

On Sunday, 12 June 1938, Mr J. B. Sainsbury requested the pleasure of the company of his employees on S.S. *Royal Eagle*. The invitation contained instructions as to times, tickets, transport, etc. prefaced by a few verses with somewhat of a sting in the last line:

> Come now, all ye social powers,
> Shed your influence o'er us;
> Crown with joy the present hours,
> Enliven those before us.

> Why the Hell should we be sad,
> Whilst on this earth we moulder?
> Rich or poor, or grave or mad,
> We every day grow older.

> Since the time will pass away,
> In spite of all our sorrow;
> Let's be blithe and gay to-day,
> And fit for work to-morrow.

As the *Royal Eagle* left Tower Pier at 9.35 a.m. Mr Sainsbury broke the House Flag at the foremast and then, from the wireless cabin, welcomed his guests and wished them 'a very enjoyable day'.

There were four sittings for lunch and tea and 'to ensure that no one gets that sinking feeling between meals there will be available during the trip ample supplies of sandwiches, pies and cakes'. Although the bar was open all the time the ship was under way, 'all members of the staff are asked to enjoy the fresh air on deck as much as possible and be ready to make the most of the four hours ashore at Margate'. There was a band on board 'but members of the Staff who can play are asked to bring their instruments with them. Those who can give a song, please bring your music.'

Finally, the excursionists were reminded 'that the mornings and evenings in June are likely to be chilly; it will, therefore, be advisable to wear warm clothing, and bring an overcoat with you'.

The British, in the sea-faring tradition, enjoyed being at sea although they seemed happy enough to disembark if the water was in the least rough. The river was calmer and conjured up images of lazy days in the sun lying in a punt or rowing energetically to reach a shady backwater. But once on the water any kind of cloud signalled possible disaster, frequent breezes might herald a squall, and once away from dry land it was not always possible to find adequate shelter. Stubbornly, it seemed, captains of pleasure steamers did not turn back. It was an admission of defeat, possibly, so if one was foolish enough to go on a pleasure trip in doubtful weather, it was pleasure you paid for and pleasure you would have whatever the conditions, and the sight of anguished passengers longing for relief from suffering was of no avail.

What are the clearest recollections of river trips between-the-wars? Surely the cold collations consisting of meats not easily identifiable but going under the names of ham and tongue, the watercress and limp salad, the warm drinks which should have been chilled served in glasses none too clean, the sound of slop buckets being emptied into the river, the sing-song on the way home accompanied by a pianist with an unerring ability to attack the wrong notes, the reflections in the water, the badinage with the lock-keepers and finally, on landing, the hesitant first few steps one took on *terra firma*.

6

Sunday School 'Trips' and Other Pleasures

'There was nothing in my childhood, only work. I never had pleasure. One day a year I went to Felixstowe along with the chapel women and children, and that was my pleasure.'

Fred Mitchell, the 85-year-old horseman quoted
in Ronald Blythe's book *Akenfield*

The happiest replies to requests for recollections of outings concerned those organised by Sunday Schools. Looking back, the weather was invariably kind. There were prayers and hymns, but unlike those that pervaded the charity outings, the Sunday School religious activity appeared to be spontaneous. Hymns were sung because the tunes were good and fitted the mood. Hymn-singing was not necessarily a 'set piece' to impress and create sympathy. Everybody voiced their happiness in song. The Sunday School outing involved the community or village. Preparations were made a long way ahead collecting money each week for the occasion. Mothers were involved in preparing food, cutting mountains of sandwiches, baking favourite cakes, the kitchens more or less taken over for the event. Meetings, discussions, prayers for good weather, last minute hitches as the day drew near were shared by all, while the children watched the proceedings with ever-mounting excitement. Perhaps father would not be able to go on the outing because it was a working day, but for mother it was a day out—a 'trip' as it was often called, but without the undesirable meaning that word has to-day. Little or no housework was done on the day. The mountains of food, drink, etc., had been taken to the church hall for loading on to the brake or charabanc, the children were in holiday mood and the pent-up excitement could now be released. Anything that was wrong could not be rectified now, everybody had contributed, everybody knew everybody, the atmosphere was as relaxed as the children would permit, and there was a determination to enjoy the day. Pensioners alive to-day who can recollect those occasions have the happiest memories of them.

Early Sunday School outings lacked the informality of those in later years, but there were dangers in travelling by train and those taking part had to be disciplined. In 1844 Sunday School male teachers in Birmingham went to the Clent Hills for a picnic, and in 1845 the Sunday School Union arranged outings for the scholars which consisted of a conducted tour round the Rotten Park Reservoir, finishing with tea in the Town Hall. A year later the Ebenezer teachers treated their scholars to a walk round the Botanical Gardens and from there to the Reservoir where two buns and a cup of milk were given to each scholar. By 1857 the Easter Tuesday treats gave place to regular outings in the summer. An innovation was introduced in 1863—a drum and fife band, which accompanied the juniors to a field at Birchfield. The seniors, for their outing to Sutton Park, were entertained by a bold brass band. So popular were these occasions that new scholars were not permitted to attend.

Sunday School children on a train excursion from Birmingham in 1845 were cautioned not to stand on the seats or lean over the sides of the open carriages, and were not to put out sticks, umbrellas or handkerchiefs. The teachers were 'respectfully' requested to remain with the children the whole time. Each scholar was given a large bun, but because of the expense teachers were to pay for these items 'upon receipt'.

On an excursion from Birmingham to Derby at about that time, the Mayor of Derby, Mr (afterwards Sir) James Allport, together with Midland Railway officials watched carefully over their young charges, and when it was found that some were missing at the time the train was due to return home, Mr Allport considerately sent a special engine to bring back the missing children so that the parents and friends would not be unduly alarmed.

Sixty members of the Battle Bridge Congregational Chapel visited Southend for a day in the summer of 1878. Ages ranged from fourteen upwards and for half of them it was their first sight of the sea. On arrival at Southend 'they were permitted by their teachers . . . to indulge in a ramble on the beach, in order to whet their appetite for a beautiful spread that awaited them, and to which they did ample justice'.

On 15 July 1880 the Langley Marish School Board in Buckinghamshire met to discuss the advisability of an outing for the children. It was proposed that the school should take advantage of the special train booked by the Royal Benefit Society for an excursion to Portsmouth. The chairman suggested

'that only the elder children of the Central School who were most deserving of conduct and regular attendance be taken to Portsmouth. The remainder with the Infants having simply a tea in the School room as heretofore. Mr. Stranson was of the opinion that excursions of our school children to the sea-side were undesirable and they encouraged habits of extravagance and restlessness and unfitted them for the position in life in which they were placed.'

The Chairman and a Mr Balfour did not share Mr Stranson's view and saw no harm in the excursion to Portsmouth. At a meeting of the Board which took place after the outing, the chairman reported that the party consisting of teachers, pupil teachers and the elder children had left Langley Station by special train at 7.50 a.m. reaching Portsmouth at 10.55. The weather was exceptionally fine and the party of seven adults and seventy-six children passed the time

'in boating and bathing, had crossed the Solent to Ryde—and had also visited the *Victory* and seen other ships of war lying in the harbour. A pleasanter excursion was never made . . . The cost of the trip amounted to £19 18s 3d which was met *by private subscription* . . . The younger children of the Central School, and the Infant children of the George Green and Horsemoor Green Schools had a substantial tea of bread and butter, cake and buns in the Central Schoolroom—150 sat down to the tea—and afterwards they amused themselves in the playground.'

There was one occasion at least when an outing—or rather the prospect of one—could be said to have demoralised not only the pupils of a school, but the staff as well. This from the log book of the Turvey Village School in Bedfordshire explains how it happened

'*7th May, 1875, Friday.* Very poor attendance indeed this morning—only 33 present. Wombell's Menagerie passed through the village a few minutes before school commenced and drew away several of the children after it. The Rector visited the school about ½ past 10 and proposed taking the children in the first two classes, that were present, to see the Menagerie. He came in at 10 minutes to 12 o'clock and informed the children that he would take them to Bedford and pay all their expenses. Fifteen children, the Master, the Sewing Mistress and the Pupil Teacher were kindly taken to Bedford to see the Show. The rest of the children had a holiday.'

This, it might be maintained by some, is the proper way to run a school. The Rector was only bowing to the inevitable and very sensibly decided to give the children a holiday when the entire staff were as eager to visit the menagerie as the pupils.

In August 1868 Mr C. C. Whitbread threw open the grounds of Southill Park to the teachers and friends of the Bunyan Meeting Sunday School from Bedford. Fifty-three people were in the party and they were conducted round the beautiful gardens. Tea was prepared on the banks of the lake and 'innocent games were indulged in, and then came a stroll to Warden Church. The party returned on the 7.3 train to Bedford having enjoyed the picnic exceedingly.'

Mrs L. Taylor of North London remembers

'those wonderful days of 1893–5 when children and teachers from our Sunday Schools in Islington clambered up into horse-drawn brakes. Some children were lucky enough to sit on the outside seats by the driver, but whether inside or outside we had a lovely view of the way we were going. Of course we chattered and waved to people, and people would look at us and shout "Good luck! Have a good day!" Soon the streets were left behind. Country roads, hedges and trees and fields took their place until we arrived at Epping Forest where we could walk or run on the grass, play games and run races . . . In 1896 we went from a London station by steam train to Southend. What an adventure that was! My first sight of the sea! . . .'

Inevitably, with the invention of the internal combustion engine outings became more ambitious because greater distances could be covered. The smells and sights from a horse-drawn brake rumbling its way along quiet country lanes became experiences of the past.

Mrs Elizabeth Tripconey at Newton St Martin, Helston in Cornwall, was born in 1894 in a small village on the Lizard Peninsular. She belonged to a family of Methodists (or Wesleyans as they were then known). At her chapel was a branch of the Temperance Society, and the great annual event was the day of the outing. The farmers lent their waggons—decorated with wild flowers and branches from the trees in the nearby woods—which were brought to the village in the evening before the big day. On the morning the horses, with their shining brasses, would be harnessed to the waggons, the seats would be placed in position and away they went.

The destination was the Lizard or Mullion, each visited on alternate years. All members of the party took lunch with them, and the Sunday School at the village visited was loaned as a base for shelter (if needed) and for cups of tea. Although it was only about twelve miles from home the feeling was that a great distance had been travelled, but it was sheer delight to jog along the lovely lanes and eventually arrive at the seaside. After roaming the cliffs and visiting the lighthouse the party set off for home at five o'clock and there, waiting at the chapel, was a lovely tea. 'Truly a red-letter day.'

When Mrs Tripconey was fourteen years of age her family moved to Plymouth and she became apprenticed to the millinery trade at a wage of one shilling a week, working from 8.30 am. to 7.30 p.m. with an hour for dinner and half-an-hour for tea. After three years she became an assistant milliner at 3s 6d a week, her wage being raised annually by that amount. She and about twenty of her colleagues had an annual day outing to the country-side and moors near Plymouth. They travelled in a cab or wagonette (also known as a Jersey car) hired from a mews in the city. The vehicle was drawn by two or four horses. 'I don't remember ever having a pouring wet day, a few showers, maybe. Then came the Great War and these delightful experiences became swallowed up in the Past!'

Mrs E. A. Lyman of Moseley, Birmingham was leader of a

Mothers' Meeting at a Wesleyan church in the Black Country from 1912 to 1927. Each year there was a Jumble Sale to provide money for the outing or 'trip' as the women called it. In 1913 they went by brake with two horses. The party gathered at the Sunday School room. There was plenty of fun and excitement when the brake arrived with its happy driver who exclaimed, 'Come on, girls, and the best-looking one can sit near me!' Another joke by the driver was covering the horses' heads with his jacket while a stout member of the party boarded the brake. 'Come on now, love,' he would cry to the good lady as she heaved herself into a seat, 'the horses would never have started if they had seen you!' Laughter all round and the 'trip' was off to a good beginning.

The brakes with all their advantages were only as safe as the horses harnessed to them. A correspondent recollects the time when she was a young teacher at the turn of the century when, on a Sunday School picnic in Sussex, the black Flemish horses drawing the brake took fright at the sight of a steam roller. The occupants might well have been pitched over the hedge into a field. The horses had to be led past the danger spot—not once, but three times—as that number of steam rollers appeared on the road as the journey proceeded.

Mr Henry Wilson of Scarborough recalls pre-1914 Sunday School outings from the little wolds village of Weaverthorpe to Scarborough.

'Strangely enough I cannot remember having anything but good weather . . . The great day started by assembling at the vicarage where we all received a shilling which promptly went into our purses. Then the impatient wait for the carrier's waggon to arrive. This vehicle, drawn by two horses had a canvas top with wooden seats along each side and a 'hatch' at the back—a wooden rack which could be let down into a horizontal position . . . There was great excitement, climbing up into the waggon in an orderly manner, supervised by the vicar . . .'

The five-mile journey up and down hill in the waggon was from the village to the station (North Eastern Railway).

'Arriving at the station the first thing we did was to place a penny into the slot machine, pull out the little drawer and there was a bar of Nestlés chocolate. Despite the fact that my parents sold chocolate in our village shop, none . . . tasted so good as this bar from the machine . . .

'The eleven-mile journey to Scarborough was full of excitement and interest. Stopping at every station, hearing the stentorian voice of the porter calling out the name of the station, the unloading and loading of the guard's van with parcels and crates of all descriptions, then the guard's whistle and off again.

'Arriving at Scarborough all made haste down to the sands. Watching the Punch and Judy show gave us the opportunity to consume the sandwich and cake which had somehow survived the journey in our pockets. The sand artist filled us with wonder, producing such masterpieces (in our eyes) using various rakes and pieces of wood to produce his designs on the perfectly smooth sand.

'Time flew, and after buying a penny ice cream, a twopenny stick of rock to take home, perhaps threepence for a present for Mother and a knife for oneself, broke and hungry we assembled for tea.'

Mrs Phyllis Willson of High Wycombe remembers the outings organised by the High Wycombe Methodist Sunday Schools just after the First World War.

'We always went by horse and cart, although the older ones walked and we smaller ones always walked *up* the hills to help the horses. My father had a small chair factory in Desborough Street and the carts used to transport the chairs were scrubbed and polished and the horses, Dick and Maggie, groomed till they shone! We always started with a procession through High Wycombe led by the Sunday School and "Band of Hope" banners, and often a band as well . . . We smaller ones sat on forms and chairs in the carts and I remember the thrill of having a silver sixpence tied in the corner of a handkerchief, to spend on sweets. There were three popular venues—West Wycombe Hill, for sledging down the hill (you hired a sledge for 2d from a cottage at the top of Church Lane), visiting the caves, non-commercialised then, and entered through a hole in the hill and lit only by a penny candle which the boys blew out when we were right inside! Sometimes we went to the grounds of Wycombe

Abbey where we explored the lake and gathered wild strawberries in the lovely hillside and then had tea and games and
"scrambles". Occasionally we visited Burnham Beeches and had
tea in the old barn, but this was rather far for the horses.'

Sadly, though, the smell of horse and countryside gave way to
the odours of petrol and urban development. There is little doubt
that the novelty of the charabanc and the feeling of speed appealed
to the children. Road was often preferable to rail because of the
number of people involved, the expense and mobility. Again, one
had to catch a train; a charabanc waited for you.

The appeal of the charabanc is described by Laurie Lee in
*Cider with Rosie** on the occasion of the Annual Slad Outing to
Weston-super-Mare:

'Then the charabancs arrived and everyone clambered on board,
fighting each other for seats . . . The charabancs were high, with
broad open seats and with folded tarpaulins at the rear, upon
which, as choirboys, we were privileged to perch and to fall off
and break our necks. We all took our places, people wrapped
themselves in blankets, horns sounded, and we were ready . . . We
swept down the thundering hills. At the speed and height of our
vehicles the whole valley took on new dimensions; woods
rushed beneath us, and fields and flies were devoured in a gulp
of air . . . We cheered everything, beast and fowl, and taunted
with heavy ironical shouts those unfortunates working in the
fields . . . Mile after rattling mile we went, under the racing sky,
flying neckties and paper kites from the back, eyes screwed in the
weeping wind. The elders, protected in front by the windscreen,
chewed strips of bacon or slept.'

On arrival at Weston-super-Mare half the village hired chairs
and bravely faced the wind, but others invaded the pier 'with our
mouths hanging open, sucking gory sticks of rock.' Then

'a long homeward drive through the red twilight . . . the engines
humming, the small children sleeping, and the young girls
gobbling shrimps. At sunset we stopped at a gaslit pub for the
men to have one more drink . . . The last home stretch: someone

* Hogarth Press

H

played a harmonica; we boys groped for women to sleep on, and slept, to the sway and sad roar of the coach and the men's thick boozy singing . . . We were home, met by lanterns—and the Outing was over.'

The petrol age did not suit everyone and a correspondent tells the story of the spinster lady, Miss H, a keen member of the church with little money who, it was decided, should be treated to an outing to Dovedale. Miss H, tall, thin and dour, had never been in a motor coach. The journey began well enough, but Miss H, who early on had said, 'Isn't it lovely?' changed after an hour to, 'I do feel ill.' The coach was stopped and Miss H was walked about gently for a few minutes before returning to the coach, which resumed its journey. Every fifteen minutes there had to be a stop for Miss H to be exercised. At Ashbourne, where the party arrived late for coffee and biscuits, Miss H exclaimed, pointing to the coach, 'I'm not going in that contraption again—not if I die here. I'll sit by the roadside and wait till you come back.' A bed-and-breakfast house was found for Miss H where she was put to bed and given cups of tea at regular intervals.

When, on the return journey, they stopped to pick up Miss H she was in a better frame of mind, but after an hour the trouble started all over again and the coach had to pull up so often that by the time the outing arrived back there was a schoolroom of anxious husbands wondering what had happened to their wives. Miss H was not asked to go on another outing; she was invited to the Christmas party instead.

Edmund Blunden in his childhood reminiscences* considered that

'the practical rewards of being a choirboy were not many, but the excursion to the seaside was looked for with huge delight. We went to the station in chilly early morning by brake, and each boy had ninepence allowed for his luxury at Hastings or Margate or some other place of piers and esplanades, besides tea at some melancholy hotel. The difficulty I found was to keep something out of my ninepence for buying a souvenir for my mother.'

* 'Country Childhood' from *Edwardian England 1901-1914* edited by S. Nowell-Smith, O.U.P.

Singing and music were important aspects of an outing. Sometimes it was merely vocal, at other times there was a band provided. Before the 1914 War, Buckfastleigh in Devon was a busy little town with woollen mills owned by a musical family named Hamlyn who formed a brass band of mill workers. On the day of the Sunday School outing the children formed a procession outside the School and, headed by the band, marched in style for half-a-mile to the railway station where the steam train, with a whistling welcome, was waiting to take the party on the outing.

Off the train went along the beautiful Dart Valley to Totnes, and from there the main line went to Teignmouth, which is where the Sunday School had their outing. The first place visited was the cockle stall, because sea-food was a great treat for country-bred children. Nobody ate so much that there was no room for tea at four o'clock in the schoolroom at St James' Church on the sea front where, in the words of someone who remembers the occasion, there was 'the most gorgeous tea' with slab cake and lots of cream and jam. The journey home began at six o'clock and the recollection is highlighted by the music of the band and the whistle of the train.

On a more scholarly occasion, the programme for the Albert Memorial, Manchester, Church Parochial Day Excursion to Oxford on Whit Friday, 20 May 1910, was divided into 'Morning Peregrination', 'Afternoon Perambulation' and 'Evening Peratetics'. Visits included Martyrs' Memorial, Site of Martyrdom, Baliol, the Clarendon Press and Bible Warehouse, with breakfast (at 9.30) and Dinner (at 2.30) at Buol's Restaurant, 21 Corn-market. Mr R. Leach's charabanc ('specially engaged') and a special Great Western Railway Train conveyed the party there and back.

Eskdalemuir is a remote parish in Dumfriesshire some thirty-five miles north of Carlisle. Early in the century the grandfather of Mr George Bell, the present postman, started annual school sports which later developed into an annual outing. The change was made in 1922 when the Sports Committee resolved to organise an outing to Lochmaben to visit one of the ruined castles of Robert the Bruce. An estimate for £8 for two charabancs was accepted to take a party of forty-six children and sixteen adults there and back. Meals, in the early days, were carried and consisted of buns and possibly a cake. Mr Bell recalls how, as a child, he and his companions thrilled at the sight of a train which occasionally flashed by the far shores of the loch. For some it was the first time they had seen a train.

Every year (except during the war years) the outing has taken place. In June 1934 the children visited Edinburgh which (according to the minute book of the Committee) 'was thoroughly enjoyed and was voted one of the best trips by all who were there. Unfortunately, the day was wet but as most of the time was spent under cover at the Zoo and later at the Fire Station things were not as bad as might have been.'

Later, outings were further afield to places such as Morecambe and Whitley Bay. There is a receipt from the Silloth Café Co. Ltd, 2, Station Road, Silloth, dated 24 June 1939, which acknowledges payment of £3 1s 8d 'to catering for 37 children to meals at 1s 8d per head'. To-day an outing costs over £100 and the money is subscribed through dances, social activities and raffles. Mr Bell, like his grandfather and father, is secretary of what is known as the 'Trip Committee'.

Mr William Foster of Driffield, North Humberside, was connected with the town's annual outings for sixty years up to 1973. In the early years the Nonconformist Sunday Schools combined for a day's excursion to Bridlington, twelve miles away. About ten days later the Church of England Scholars would have a similar excursion. This arrangement continued until 1921, when the Nonconformists experienced a day of almost continuous rain. On the return the excursionists were met by prominent tradesmen, who offered to collect sufficient funds in the town for another excursion that year and it was duly arranged.

The same offer was made by the tradesmen the year following, provided the Nonconformists joined forces with the Church of England for an excursion. This was achieved, and ever since 1922 (except for the war years) a joint excursion has taken place. Eventually the now defunct Urban District Council looked after the financial side and the Sunday School Committee made the arrangements.

At one time a bag of buns for each child was bought in Driffield and conveyed to Bridlington by road and distributed there about lunch-time from two centres in the town. The children were reluctant to leave the sands to collect their buns, so instead, 6d (now 2½p) was given to each child with the railway ticket. The age limits for free tickets etc. used to be from three to sixteen if attending Sunday Schools, or three to fourteen if not. This rule was, in later years, altered to three to sixteen for all children. In the years of the steam train, when most children had only one day at the seaside, the excursions catered for as many as ten or eleven hundred children and over 600 adults. Two luggage vans were provided on each train and all prams and push chairs were carried without cost. Due to more leisure, and families having cars, the numbers going on the outing decreased, but surprisingly in the last two or three years there has been a slight annual increase.

Mrs A. B. Horner of Otley, Yorkshire, was from 1930 to 1939 head of a small school, Stainburn (now closed), with about thirty-five children. There was no shop in the district so she sold sweets and held whist drives to raise money to take the children with a parent on an annual outing. For the year of George VI's coronation they went to Liverpool and were shown round a liner in dock at New Brighton. Generally everybody took a packed lunch to eat at midday, and a high tea was arranged for about five o'clock. After tea the journey home was via Chester, where the party had a good sight of the street decorations.

Miss R. F. Claughton of Silsden, Keighley, West Yorkshire, has happy memories of choir outings prior to 1939. In the small West Riding towns and villages the Methodist tradition was very strong and the chapels were the centre of social activity. In Miss Claughton's village of some 5,000 inhabitants there were three Methodist chapels and each had an annual choir outing. The choir and organist and as many wives, husbands and friends as could be accommodated in an open charabanc, assembled for the outing at 7 a.m. when a hymn or two was sung in the centre of the village. For a young man or woman to invite a member of the opposite sex to a choir outing was almost tantamount to an engagement.

The singing over, the young people made a dash for the seats at the back of the charabanc, their elders moving more sedately to the front. Perhaps the outing would be to Ingleton and at each stop on the way the choir would sing an anthem or two and a couple of hymns. 'In those less sophisticated days we were generally applauded and even asked for some special tune by onlookers,' comments Miss Claughton.

On arrival, a good lunch, a free afternoon, and no stops after dark on the return journey, but fish and chips were available for those who wanted them. 'Coming gently home after dark someone would generally strike up a hymn—I have happy memories of coming through the lovely countryside, with a magnificent sunset, singing (and meaning) "The Day Thou Gavest, Lord, has ended".'

Back in the village again, no matter what the time, the choir sang two more songs before going to their homes, and 'it was a point of honour that we should all be in chapel next morning', writes Miss Claughton. The choir outing was, according to her, 'one of the highlights of the summer. In my recollection it always seems to have been a fine day.'

As a brash twelve-year-old in 1936, Mr A. J. Taylor, now lecturer in Production Engineering at a technical college in Shropshire, recollects cycling with a friend in the long summer evenings, visiting remote Lincolnshire fen farms to make cheeky appeals for funds to help finance the Sunday School Outing from Sutton Bridge to Hunstanton, some twenty-eight miles away. Each year the outing was on a Wednesday, everyone of importance went on it, and it meant a day off from school. Mothers paying their own fare, infants, grandmothers, and a few men (because it was early closing day) would congregate at the station on the morning of the outing at 'something after nine'. Mr Taylor describes the outing and the scene with a proper sense of occasion, and in his own words brings back memories of those between-the-wars years, the fashions, the attitudes, the excitement of simple pleasures—and even the smells.

'For at least an hour previously the straggling, laden families would have walked along the Main Road towards the station . . . Entire familes, too, had travelled to the station on bicycles; small bikes for those old enough to ride bikes with saddles on the cross-bar, some with baskets on the back in which tiny infants lolled like the offspring of latterday Red Indians. Bicycles that were now parked untidily by the diamond woodwork of the station-yard fence.

'The sun always seemed to shine on that crowded platform. It smelled of shell-fish, newsprint, disinfectant—and the lime-encrusted urinal at the far end. It was too late in the year for daffodils and tulips but there were a few cardboard boxes of cut flowers stacked on a trolley waiting for the Peterborough train. And a few early punnets of strawberries. There was a marvellous happy sort of chaos—trippings over push-chairs, buckets and spades; a faded last-year's Union Jack, baskets and string bags holding sandwiches and the towels and costumes for bathing and paddling . . .

'For their day out the males old enough to wear long trousers would display white shirts, braces, and freshly-whitened plim-solls—or brown sandals with perforated uppers and crêpe soles. As the time approached the late arrivals would join the jostling to get a good seat. Familes manœuvred and mothers shepherded in the hope of cornering a compartment to themselves.

'The train would be too long for the platform; as it approached there would be frantic snatchings and shrieks . . . When one half of the train had been filled to bursting point it would "draw up". The fierce little gradient with its sharp bend leading up to the bridge would tax the engine. There would be a great spinning of wheels and escape of steam . . . Every window in every coach would be wound down. Children squabbled over the corner seats. Handkerchiefs and hands waved excitedly. The stragglers took their seats in the second half of the train. They joined those who had deliberately held back . . . the wise ones knew that the train turned round at Lynn. The rear end would get into Hun-stanton first—a precious six-coach lengths nearer the ticket barrier . . .

'At Heacham we could really see the sea . . . We eased into Hunstanton Station and gathered up our baskets and gear. We spilled out on to the platform . . .

'Outside the station we poured on to the Green—elegant sloping lawns in front of the Sandringham Hotel . . . Deck chairs for adults, raincoats for children if the sand was damp. The first paddle, then bathing costumes on and really into the sea if the water was warm enough. Grandmas tucked dresses in to knicker legs and displayed varicose veins and massive, blotchy, bleached thighs . . .

'Then we had boiled ham sandwiches, bottle of lemon barley or yellow lemonade made from two ounces of crystals bought from the corner-shop. We made mammoth sand-castles; there were long walks to the water's edge for buckets which spilled half their contents on the way back. Vague panic as one's particular family . . . receded into the distant blur of countless families squatting below the promenade. High-stepping overloaded donkeys crossed over our tracks.'

The older ones sampled the open-air bathing pool and the amusement park. Crazy Golf was good value, Penny-on-the-Mat (or Helter Skelter) was dramatic, the Ghost Train disturbing, the Dodg'em expensive. No visit was complete without a visit to the gardens, and a look at the pier had to suffice as entry would have been too much of a financial strain.

'The final ritual would be a visit to the shops in the town, where Mums marvelled at the very high seaside prices . . . Getting to the station early was surely an adult ploy, and we were never first. On the way we had time to feed coins into the slot-machines: we stamped out our names on little aluminium strips, being very careful not to exceed the twenty-six letters allowed. The train of carriages was already in the station. The westerly sun would scorch and dazzle and we would pull down the blinds in the compartment. There would be sticky fingers everywhere, the result of handling rock, candy floss, oranges. Last drops of lemonade would be squeezed from near-empty bottles. Bananas and apples helped to stave off the effect of raging thirst . . . On the way back towards Lynn a window seat would sometimes give a fleeting glance of rabbits disappearing into their burrow. There were rhododendrons to admire, and the smell of pinewoods near Sandringham.

'At Sutton Bridge there were fathers and relatives waiting on the platform to greet us . . . Home again. Drinks and more drinks. Cold cream to soothe sunburned shoulders. Will we be going again next year?'

That was in 1936. Perhaps Mr Taylor enjoyed three more outings, but at the time nobody knew for certain.

7

Exhibitions
and Other Events

'An "exhibition" might profitably have been made of the way in
which our poor were housed, to teach the admiring foreign visitor
some of the dangers that beset the path of the vaunted new era.'
G. M. Trevelyan on the Great Exhibition of 1851,
in *English Social History*

There is a fairly wide category of outings and excursions which do
not fit easily into any specific pattern, and included are those
occasions when people travelled in groups to take part in a specific
activity and not just to laze by the sea or pick flowers in a field.
Visiting exhibitions, for example, when the firms showing considered it would be uplifting for their employees to see the company
stand and, at the same time, make the occasion a jollification.
There were numerous trade exhibitions in the nineteenth century
when British industry was flexing its industrial muscles and
wanted all the world to see. The best-known was the 1851 Exhibition which, from the excursion aspect, was a resounding success.
As many as 165,000 came from the provinces to visit the exhibition
under the auspices of Thomas Cook alone.

Less well known and fascinating in its way was the twentieth-
century British Empire Exhibition at Wembley in 1924 'designed
to display the natural resources of the various countries within the
Empire and the activities, industrial and social, of their peoples'.
Thus the official catalogue, and it was achieved by erecting un-
imaginative buildings to house the exhibits. By then, of course,
conveying numerous groups of people from one place to another
had become commonplace. This was not the case in 1851.

It had been estimated that anything from three to five million people would visit the 1851 Exhibition and the *Illustrated London News* in their issue of 21 September 1850, some months before the exhibition opened, pointed out that

'Already the working classes in Manchester, Liverpool, Sheffield, Birmingham, the Potteries, and the great iron districts between Glasgow and Airdrie, as well as other places, have commenced laying by their weekly pence to form a fund for visiting the metropolis during the Great Exhibition of 1851; and it is not the least gratifying of the many pleasant associations connected with that event, that it has been the means of eliciting such a praise-worthy organisation among the working classes. Were it not for cheap excursion trains, this great source of amusement and instruction would have been unattainable by hard-working poverty, and the Exhibition would have lost one of its great attractions.'

Some visitors came from so far away that a 'day' excursion was not possible, the usual stay in London being from three days to a week. Accommodation had to be provided. This was a matter left to private enterprise and in many instances the accommodation supplied was unsatisfactory and the prices charged exorbitant, but the Royal Commissioners established a register in which the names and addresses of those willing to let rooms were included. This, it was considered, would be helpful to the working classes and artisans.

One of the establishments registered was that of Mr Thomas Harrison at Ranelagh Road, Pimlico. The building—about a mile from the exhibition—was close to Pimlico Pier, where steamboats arrived from the City every ten minutes. It occupied two acres, was surrounded by roads on three sides 'in a perfectly airy situation, and admirably ventilated'. There were two sleeping rooms, 25,000 feet in area, and two dormitories of half that area, all planned to accommodate a thousand people a night. Each lodger had his own bedroom (and the key to it), which was partitioned 'thus assuring perfect privacy'. Wardens were on duty and the dormitories were well lit by gas at night. There was a dining room, reading room and smoking room. A news-room plentifully supplied with newspapers, magazines 'and all publications relating to the Exhibition and other sights of London, free of charge'. In the smoking room (which was apart from the main building) a band played every evening free of charge, while on top of the building was a lantern 1,500 ft. square from which visitors obtained an excellent view of the river and 'the surrounding country'. Hot rolls were baked on the premises and people paid for what they wanted to eat.

'It is believed that a very decent breakfast may be had for 4d or 6d, and a good dinner for 8d; and there will be no lack of provisions . . . The price for lodging will be 1s 3d per night, including attendance, and soap, towels, and every convenience for ablution. Boots will be cleaned for a penny a pair; the barber will attend to the heads and chins of the visitors as cheaply; and there will be a room for luggage, the charge for stowage in which will be one halfpenny. A surgeon is to attend daily at nine o'clock. An omnibus will run between this Mechanics' Home and the Exhibition, the fare by which will only be 1d. . . . The utmost liberty will be given to the lodgers, but care will be taken that no one shall be suffered to create an annoyance, and there will be persons there ready to take care of those who, through drink or otherwise, should forget for a time to take care of themselves.'

The South Eastern Railway Company with the co-operation of the Northern Railway Company of France brought visitors from Paris, the journey taking eleven hours. A visitor from Marseilles would reach London in forty-six hours and the cost of a return first-class ticket was £6. The price of an excursion ticket from Leeds and back allowing for a three-week stay in London was 15s first class, 10s second class and 5s third class, but according to the First Report of the Commissioners for the Exhibition, 'from the class of persons who travelled by these trains, it was evident that ordinary third-class passengers were found with second, and very frequently with first-class tickets'.

The 'shilling' day at the Exhibition drew as many as 70,000 visitors. A Frenchman observed that it was the day

'for country people, who arrive in their rustic dresses, with their wives, their children, and provisions. The railways bring them to London at reduced fares, and at the station they take large waggons, which bring them to the Exhibition. Caravans full of them are thus encountered in the streets. Whole parishes sometimes come, headed by their clergymen. The colonels of regiments send their soldiers, and the admirals their sailors. Not less worthy of observation are the hundreds of charity children, in their blue dress with yellow stockings, that are frequently met marching in rank and file.'

Schools sent their pupils—Christ's Hospital being responsible for 900. Eighty boys and girls from Messrs Fawbert and Barnard's School, Harlow, visited the exhibition. 'Before starting the juveniles gave three hearty cheers for their kind benefactors, full of glee in anticipation of the high treat they were about to witness.' On return to Harlow the party was met by the Harlow band, which played while the children marched from the station to the town 'when they all joined in singing the National Anthem and then departed to their respective homes'.

Masters sent their servants, manufacturers their workpeople, bankers and merchants their staff, tradesmen their assistants, farmers their labourers. Lord Willoughby d'Eresby, it was said, rented a house in London to accommodate his tenants. A workman left Huddersfield in the night of 22 July for the exhibition paying 5s for his third-class return fare. In his pocket were sandwiches and a shilling; the latter he parted with at the entrance. He ate his sandwiches in the building, drank water from a fountain and returned to Huddersfield within forty hours and went back to work. The total outlay of 6s for such an outing was cheap even by 1851 standards! No liquor was sold at the exhibition—it was 'dry'—so the temptation to spend money was not very great, which no doubt prompted the *Punch* cartoon headed SCENE— EXHIBITION REFRESHMENT ROOM: Two rather rough characters are depicted at the bar. 'Pint o' Beer, Miss, Please,' says one. The Miss replies, 'Don't keep it. You can have a strawberry ice and a wafer.' A look of utter gloom can be observed on the faces of the two rough characters.

The brunt of this vast influx of visitors had been borne by the railways and from the experience gained the railway companies were to stride forward in the realm of excursion traffic. As for the people of Britain, the opportunities that had been given to them

THE GREAT EXHIBITION, 1851.

TO THE

Working Classes OF BEVERLEY.

In consequence of a Circular having been sent by the Executive Committee in London, to the Local Committee in the Country, importing that the facilities proposed to be afforded by the Railway Companies, for enabling the Working Classes to visit the Exhibition, will be confined exclusively to such as are associated in Travelling Clubs, formed for that especial purpose, it is necessary that immediate steps should be taken for the formation of such Travelling Associations.

I do therefore hereby convene a PUBLIC MEETING to be held at the GUILD-HALL, in Beverley, on WEDNESDAY, the First day of January next, at SEVEN o'Clock in the Evening, for the purpose of adopting and carrying out such resolutions as may be deemed expedient, to enable the Subscribers to visit the Exhibition.

The following is an Extract from the Circular referred to

That in order to encourage the early formation of "Subscription Clubs" in the Country, to enable the labouring classes to travel to London and back during the Exhibition of 1851. the Railway Companies should now undertake to convey all persons so subscribing to local clubs at a single railway fare for both journeys, up and down, which shall in no case exceed the existing fare by Parliamentary Trains for the journey in one direction, with an abatement for distances, subject to the following conditions:—

That in respect of journeys to London, the first 100 miles shall always be charged as 100 miles, and where the distance shall exceed 100 miles, an allowance in the fare be made on the following scale:—

For the first excess 100 miles, 1-5th, or 20 per cent. be allowed
For the second excess 100 miles, 3-10ths, or 30 per cent be allowed.
For the third excess 100 miles, 2-5ths, or 40 per cent. be allowed.
For the Fourth excess 100 miles, ½ or 50 per cent. be allowed.

Thus for instance :—

A distance of 150 miles will be paid for as 140 miles,
,, 200 ,, ,, 180 ,,
,, 300 ,, ,, 250 ,,
,, 400 ,, ,, 310 ,,
,, 500 ,, ,, 360 ,,

and in like proportion between the respective distances.

That 250 passengers for the whole journey must be secured, in order to engage a special train, the hour of arrival in London being made as convenient as possible for the Excursionists, and the time of departure for the return journey being previously arranged according to circumstances, but in no case to exceed six days from that of arrival.

That the Railway Companies shall not be required to bring up any Subscription Clubs before the 1st of July, 1851, nor until the admittance to the Exhibition shall have been reduced to 1s., and then only at such time as may be specially fixed according to the general convenience of each Company.

PENNOCK TIGAR, MAYOR.

Guild-Hall, 24th December, 1850.

M. ELLIS, PRINTER, POST-OFFICE, TOLL-GAVEL, BEVERLEY.

to travel long distances cheaply to see the wondrous exhibition revealed a world unknown to them. There in the massive Crystal Palace were goods and machinery that they had made in the grime-infested towns of the industrial Midlands and the North. Not only that, there it all was for all to see! They observed the foreigners that flocked to the exhibition and learnt from various sources the praise that was bestowed on the quality and workmanship of the exhibits. They had every right to feel proud, for without the workers the exhibition could not have been mounted. Additionally, their beloved Queen was closely linked with its success.

There was a spate of other exhibitions to follow, but they were limited in scope. In 1862 a special visit was arranged by Huntley & Palmer for their employees to see the firm's display at the London Exhibition. The partners paid for the 1s admission as well as the fare of 2s per head in a special train. A total of 1,084 employees sat down to tea. One incident occurred. A young man in the packing department, earning 16s a week, was reimbursed 30s out of the firm's Trade Charges for damage to his girl's dress at the exhibition.

In 1883 the South Eastern Railway Company, on receipt of a guaranteed 250 passengers, was prepared to run a special train from Rye to London for the Great International Fisheries Exhibition. An appeal for people to take coupons for tickets was made by Francis Bellingham, Mayor, and A. W. Smith, President of the Rye District Commercial Associates, 'as this will be the only opportunity of having the advantage of a special train at Excursion rates' which were 10s first-class return; 5s third class.

On 14 October 1911, Ferranti Ltd organised a London trip for employees to visit the Electrical Exhibition at Olympia, where the company had stands 102 and 113. An early start—just after midnight—from Manchester and district ensured arrival at St Pancras at about six o'clock. The excursionists were directed to Slater's Restaurant at 142 Strand 'by bus from St Pancras Church (five minutes walk from St Pancras Station along Euston Road) to the Gaiety Theatre, Fare 1d, or on the Piccadilly Tube from King's Cross to Covent Garden Station, which is five minutes walk of the restaurant'. Breakfast at Slaters was at 8 a.m. sharp, but as Covent Garden Market was only five minutes away it 'could be visited before breakfast'. The breakfast menu was Fried Fillet of Fish;

Grilled Chop or Grilled Ham and Eggs; Bread and Butter; Preserves; Tea and Coffee; Rolls.

Dinner was at Olympia in the Pillar Restaurant at one o'clock. The menu: Consommé en Tasse; Roast Mutton and Mint Sauce; Roast Beef, Yorkshire Pudding; French Beans, Potatoes; Apple Tart and Cream; Charlotte Russe; Bread, Butter and Cheese.

Seventy-three years after the 1851 Exhibition, the British Empire Exhibition took place at Wembley. It was a tribute to the Empire which had contributed so much to victory in the Great War. From an excursion point of view the circumstances were very different. The brunt was not borne by the railways; the charabanc travelled the network of roads covering Britain, and the official guide to the exhibition—almost an afterthought—pointed out that 'for the private motor owner who has brought his car to Wembley there is a Car Park outside the South West Entrance'.

Seventy-three years before people, due to the railways, were beginning to travel from the villages and towns in which they had been confined for most of their lives. In 1924 travel was an established way of life. The war had seen to that. Visitors to the Empire Exhibition did not necessarily come to see London but to tour the British Empire. It *could* be done in a day. After seeing New Zealand, Malaya, Sarawak, Australia, 'walk', recommends the official guide, 'through Canada, through the West African Walled City, to East Africa and South Africa. Then follow the road past Ceylon, Malta, and the Hong Kong Street with its Chinese people and produce.'

Educationally the exhibition was important and there were few schools that did not acknowledge the fact. Industry responded by sending their workpeople, because many companies had close ties with the Empire and had displays in the Palaces of Industry or Engineering. It was unkind of the *Illustrated Sunday Herald* of 22 June 1924 to comment, 'However much it may disappoint the educationists, it must be admitted that almost every one headed for the Amusement Park.' To be fair, this referred to a specific firm's outing, but the shouts and screams from those enjoying the switchback, 'The Frolic' or the 'Grand National Switchback' in the Amusement Park could be heard by the more serious-minded intent on studying the Prince of Wales sculptured in butter in the Canadian Pavilion.

'Works all over the country are closing down for the day,' reported the *Evening Standard* on 12 June, 'to send the whole of their employees to Wembley'. These included 2,000 from Mardon, Son and Hall from Bristol; 3,000 from the Dunlop Rubber Company, Birmingham; 2,000 from Bass, Ratcliffe & Gretton, Burton; 2,500 from Guest, Keen & Nettlefolds, Birmingham; 3,000 from the Metropolitan Vickers; 2,000 from J. S. Fry & Son, Bristol; 4,400 from Huntley & Palmer, Reading. William Gossages & Son Ltd sent 540 employees from Widnes.

On 30 June Lever Bros hired five special trains for Wembley and a similar expedition was arranged for the four succeeding Mondays until the whole 14,000 had seen the Exhibition. Wives of employees were included, and children from the ages of nine to sixteen. The firm had an advertisement in the official guide of a panoramic view of Port Sunlight, welcoming visitors to their stand—No. 30 in the Chemical Section—'where the world famous products of Port Sunlight—the home of Sunlight Soap, Lifebuoy Soap, Lux, Vim, Twink—can be seen'. Visitors were told to be sure to visit the Sunlight Cinema in the Amusements Park. This contribution to *Port Sunlight News* signed 'A Planter's Clerk' throws an interesting light on the financial circumstances of some of those who visited the exhibition:

'When my turn came to join the Wembley picnic, I was faced with three problems. The first was: How could I get up in time to catch the 5.45 a.m. Blue Train? The second was: How could I "do" the Exhibition in a day? And the third was: How can I spend my three shillings in the most profitable manner? First: called my landlady. Writer asked one lady how she managed to get up so early. "Why, you silly, I simply put my guide book, badge, railway ticket and other accessories under my pillow, banged my head five times on the pillow—and woke up at five." Second: he found he could do the exhibition in a day. Third: spent a shilling to see replica of tomb of Tutankamen. Balance of money on some ham sandwiches, and something to drink.'

Another big invasion was 5,500 employees from Boots. Eight special trains left Nottingham at 5.45 a.m. on Saturday, 21 June. The weather was fine and everybody was in good spirits. The outing cost the firm £5,000 and was organised with, it appears, military precision by Major T. Knowles of the company's Welfare Department. Each train was in charge of a steward and there were first aid compartments in charge of qualified nurses. One employee wearily commented, 'Colony after Colony we inspected until within an hour of our departure, for relaxation, we hied to the

One Way of Writing "Wembley."

The artful arrangement of Lever advertisements by which one excursionist records his experiences.

I

Amusement Park, leaving just in comfortable time to catch the homeward train.' But for May Allen of the Packed Goods (Stock) Office, then fifteen years of age, the Exhibition was something of an inspiration:

'The Exhibition is truly a wonderful place, and one of its objects has been achieved; it has made us realise what we owe to our Colonists, the courageous men and women who braved the danger of both known and unknown lands, in the love of their mother country. They all deserve thanks from the Empire, and we cannot think of what would happen if we had no colonies to provide us with the many materials which we need and cannot provide ourselves. The 21st June, 1924, will never be forgotten by any Boots' employees . . .'

Some fifty years later these words have a nostalgic ring about them.

The employees of Faire Bros & Co. Ltd travelled in two special trains on Saturday, 27 September, to Wembley. They left London Road (LMS) Leicester at just after six o'clock in the morning, arriving at St Pancras about two hours later. In a leaflet issued to each employee it was pointed out that 'the following are places of special interest at the Exhibition, and it is strongly recommended that you visit them:—H.M. Government, Australia, Canada, New Zealand, India, Palace of Engineering, the African States.'

Then followed instructions about the closing times and where-abouts of cloak rooms, the existence of Red Cross stations 'in case of sudden illness', advice if lost—'ask a policeman', warnings about not giving up an entrance ticket until the exhibition had been entered, a reminder that extra would have to be paid if employees went by any other route than the one specified to and from the exhibition, a reminder not to forget (a) railway ticket, (b) entrance ticket, and that although there were ample opportunities for meals in the exhibition grounds, 'it is advisable not to go just at "rush" hours, and enquiry should always be made as to prices'. A director of the firm to-day suggests that, on looking back, it does indicate how little sense the organisers gave their employees credit for in those days!

There is a society for everything in Britain. No matter what subject is raised, forward comes some organisation which has interested members who need protecting, or want to get things changed. By the same token the railway companies endeavoured to cater for every interest, and if sufficient numbers of people could be collected together, a special train was made available and an 'excursion' arranged.

On Tuesday, 23 June 1857, in connection with the Manchester Exhibition of Art Treasures, it was arranged by the Shropshire Provident Society to hire a train that ran direct to the exhibition building. Tickets included the journey to and from Manchester as well as admission to the exhibition at a cost of 5s to non-members of the Society, while members (each of whom might take either a parent, wife, child, brother or sister on the same terms) 4s each. The Refreshment Department at the exhibition did much to sustain the excursionists by offering for dinner, joint of beef (roast or boiled), 1s; plate of meat and bread, 7d; small ditto, 5d; cup of tea or coffee, 3d; ginger beer, 3d; glass of beer or porter, 2d, so it was cheaper to view the exhibits having imbibed an intoxicating drink than quench the thirst with harmless beverages.

The London, Chatham & Dover Railway, catering for cricket enthusiasts, ran a cheap excursion to the Crystal Palace ('and London') on 27 September 1880, enabling them to see the Great Cricket Match between the Australians and the Players. The train stopped at Penge, which was within five minutes walk of the Garden Entrance to the Crystal Palace, and at Victoria Station for those not interested in cricket but just wanting to visit London. The return third class fare from Dover to Penge or London was 5s.

'Caerphilly Castle—the Home of King Henry III' announced the Taff Vale Railway poster of 1889. An excursion train left Pontypridd at 11 a.m. and returned from Caerphilly at 7.45 in the evening. Tickets had to be bought beforehand because none would be issued on the morning of the excursion. Excursionists were invited to explore the ruins and the Pentrych Brass Band was in attendance 'assisted by several Artistes to entertain'. Tea was available, the price of which was included in the fare of 1s 6d for adults and 1s for children (under 12).

The British loved a good hanging. Ghoulish observers flocked to the gallows to watch less fortunate beings 'drop' in the legally accepted manner of that time. The abolition of public hanging in

1868 must have robbed the railway companies of a profitable source of income. When at Liverpool in September 1849, J. Gleeson Wilson, convicted of murdering Mrs Ann Hinrichson, her two sons and a servant, was hanged at Kirkdale Gaol, 80–90,000 people arrived to witness the scene, many coming by excursion train. 'A few minutes before twelve,' reports the *Nottingham Journal* of 21 September, 'Wilson was led forth to the drop . . . Scarcely three minutes elapsed e'er the bolt was drawn and the poor man died after a few but severe struggles.'

Earlier, in 1840, the murderer of Mr Norway, a citizen of Wadebridge, created considerable interest locally. Consequently the Bodmin and Wadebridge Railway ran three special trains to Bodmin so that those living in Wadebridge could view the hanging of William Lightfoot, the convicted man. Almost half the population of Wadebridge—1,100 people—took advantage of the facilities offered, and as the jail adjoined the Bodmin railway depot, passengers were able to see the spectacle in comfort without having to leave their carriages.

The Londonderry and Lough Swilly Railway advertised a Grand Evening Fête at Gwynn's of illuminations and fireworks on 8 September 1886, the special train leaving Derry (Midland Quay) at 10.10 p.m. for Buncrana, calling at intermediate stations to pick up more passengers. Nearly forty years later, on Sunday, 22 July 1923, the same railway company issued posters inviting excursionists to view the consecration of the Bishop-elect of Raphoe at Letterkenny.

When, in August 1844, the Earl of Zetland laid the foundation stone of the monument in memory of the Earl of Durham on Penster Hill, Northumberland, a special train left Gateshead, Sunderland and Shields carrying those wishing to attend the ceremony.

In November 1852 the Great Northern Railway arranged for excursions to the lying in state and funeral of the Duke of Wellington. A special train left Leeds at 10.15 a.m., stopping at Wakefield, Sheffield and intermediate stations, arriving at King's Cross at six in the evening. The return fare from Leeds was 37s 6d, first class, 20s 'covered' car, and children under 12½ half-price.

On a happier note Thomas Cook organised, in 1853, an excursion by the Midland Railway from Gloucester to Scotland, 'this being the first time he had the honour of conducting a party of excursionists via Gretna Green, and if any demand is made by ladies and gentlemen of the party for the services of Mr Linton or Mr Murray (the "Gretna parsons"), the special train shall be detained, to enable them to terminate "single blessedness" '.

In 1860 the line to Aboyne was opened and the Deeside Railway Company, conscious of the fact that Queen Victoria travelled on the line from Edinburgh to Balmoral, advertised excursion tickets from Aberdeen to Aboyne in order to see Her Majesty arrive there. The train left Aberdeen at 11.15 and on arrival the excursionists joined spectators from the neighbourhood. Consequently there was a considerable crowd to acclaim the Queen.

In 1911 special trains ran between Euston, Leighton and Bletchley for hunting enthusiasts to attend Lord Rothschild's Staghounds, the Whaddon Chase, and the Bicester Foxhounds. Football supporters of Bolton Wanderers and Manchester City travelled in a single train leaving Leeds Central at 1.30 in the morning arriving (via Holbeck and Wakefield) at King's Cross at 6.19 a.m. The date was 23 April 1904, and in the manner of football enthusiasts in later years they wandered round London visiting such attractions as the London Hippodrome (then a circus) and Madame Tussaud's before attending the match at Crystal Palace. The handbill announcing the occasion was in the shape of a football and was issued jointly by the Great Northern and North Eastern Railways.

In another chapter there have been examples of employees visiting the home of the head of a firm for the annual outing. This could be attributed to benevolent paternalism or a genuine wish that employees should spend the day in pleasant surroundings at the invitation of the employer. Some employers no doubt thought that it brought worker and master in closer touch, especially when it was seen that trouble had been taken to make the day a success and that the employer and his family were acting as hosts. The more cynical might comment that it was cheaper to do it that way than have to spend money at an hotel for a slap-up meal for some hundreds of people. Comparatively few employers had homes in spacious grounds of sufficient size to entertain a multitude of people.

From the employee's point of view a day spent at the home—but not necessarily *in* the home—of his employer was a mixed blessing, Employers who had the facilities for such entertaining were unlikely to be in day-to-day touch with any but senior management. To the man or woman on the shop floor he was a figurehead. Nevertheless, the employee was possibly curious to visit a world so outside the scope of his attainment. On the other hand, in less enlightened days, a degree of opulent living by the head of a large company was considered natural enough in a world so blatantly inhabited by 'haves' and 'have-nots'. Unlike the outing at which you could take off your tie or loosen the corsets, an invitation to an employer's home meant no relaxation in attire or—even more important—behaviour. It was easy enough on the way to Clacton or Blackpool to over-indulge in drink, steal a kiss, pinch a bottom and other pleasant but harmless diversions, but such behaviour would certainly not be countenanced in the grounds of an employer's home where everyone walked decorously down garden paths admiring the flowers, strolled sedately on the lawns, played nice, quiet organised games, and 'took' tea in the marquees, balancing sandwiches perilously on saucers. Once it might be tolerable, even enjoyable, but annually it could become something of a strain.

Every year the employees of *The Times* visited Hever Castle, the home of their employer, Major Astor. A booklet issued for the occasion of the outing on 13 June 1925 contains a loose colour reproduction of Holbein's portrait at the Castle of Anne Boleyn which could easily be framed. Transport arrangements included the Special Train Service (six trains) to Hever for which blue and red tickets were issued and these, it was pointed out, 'should be exchanged at the special window at the Main Line Booking Office, Victoria Station (Brighton Railway), labelled "Book Here for *The Times* Party"'. Details were given of the ordinary train service (for which the tickets for the special trains were not valid), and it was to be noted that the 11.15 was for first-class passengers only, although the train 'will accommodate 3rd-class passengers by special arrangement if required'. On arriving at Hever Station there were omnibuses waiting to convey guests 'to the domain entrance'.

A page in the brochure headed 'General Information for Guests' referred the visitor to the double-spread map in the centre on which cloak rooms, lost property 'bureaux', luncheon marquee, embulance points ('sections of *The Times* ambulance Corps and of the St. John Ambulance Brigade, will be in attendance. Dr. Wilson of *The Times*, will be present during the day') were marked by numbers. The Band of the Green Howards played selections from 'Madame Pompadour', 'No, No, Nanette', 'The Pirates of Penzance', 'Katja the Dancer', and 'Rose Marie' during the day, first in the neighbourhood of the luncheon marquee, and later in the Italian Garden. Dance music was played for two hours from 4.30 p.m.

There were two sittings for lunch for the 3,300 people present and the menu included cold salmon, cold chicken, tongue, ham, strawberry melba with home-made lemonade, claret cup and ale to quench the thirst. For tea, from 4.15 there was white and brown bread-and-butter, *pains fourrés*, almond and Dundee cake, various biscuits, assorted French pastry, ham and tongue with lettuce. And if the spirits should flag there were light refreshments of orangeade, lemonade, pastries, cakes and ices served from half past two.

Activities to entertain the guests were numerous. A treasure hunt, tennis and golf, a photograph competition (a dark room for changing plates being available); rowing (with the request that owing to the number of guests, boats would not be taken out for more than thirty minutes at a time); swimming (towels provided), and dancing on the green. Lady Violet Astor presented the prizes to the winners of the competitions, every lady received a box of chocolates and every man a packet of cigarettes. The cost of it all must have been staggering, and the organisation that enabled so many people to be conveyed from London, fed so sumptuously and entertained, was of almost military precision. And if it rained? Proceed, please, to the shelter tent for dancing and where also *The Times* Amateur Dramatic Society had 'most kindly volunteered to give an entertainment'.

The blue ticket guests caught special trains leaving Hever Station between 6.40 and 7.30; red tickets between 7.47 and 8.30, the last special train arriving at Victoria at 9.20 Most of the guests were confined to the grounds, and only those who received special tickets were admitted to the Castle at specified times. 'In view of the risk of fire gentlemen are particularly requested not to smoke while in the Castle.' The idea that one of the ladies might long for a quick drag was unthinkable.

Talking to members of *The Times* staff who attended this

extraordinary occasion annually reveals a mixture of feelings and attitudes. To some it became an annual penance. A ticket to enter the Castle was a symbol of success and acceptance, but the majority never received the key to that particular heaven.

' "Sweet" Athletes' and 'Walking Makes the Heart "Fondant" ' punned the local paper when the Clarnico Sports and Social Club went on their outing, which consisted of a Ladies' Annual Walk from the company's Stratford, London works to Epping. Clarnico was the trade name of Clarke, Nicholls and Coombs, sweet manufacturers, and on a particular outing that took place on 21 May 1929 forty-seven competitors started from the Main Yard Gate at 8 a.m. sharp. Each competitor was permitted one attendant who was not allowed to join before Leyton Town Hall. The attendant might offer the competitor refreshment but not assist in any other way. The winner was presented with a silver cup by the wife of a director, and the cup could be held for a year. Each competitor finishing the course within three hours of the start received a medal. The route, after Leyton Town Hall, was Snaresbrook, Woodford, Loughton Fountain to Epping Church, a distance of fourteen miles. At two o'clock two charabancs arrived to bring the competitors back to Stratford.

The coal mining community had their outings and although in pre-nationalisation days the colliery owners did not neglect the social side of the miner's life, it is difficult to obtain information about such occasions. There are instances of outings that were organised at the initiative of the miners themselves.

The annual picnic of the Northumberland Miners' Association Gala Day was good value for money and combined pleasure and politics in equal measure. One held at Blyth Links on Saturday, 21 July 1883, consisted of a Public Meeting 'when Addresses will be delivered . . . on Political and Social Questions'. The speakers included Messrs C. Bradlaugh, MP, T. Burt, MP, John Morley, MP and others. Later tea was provided in a large marquee. Prices for males, 1s; females, 9d and children under twelve, 6d. After tea, it was announced, a ball would be held, admission 1s per couple, and it was promised that 'an efficient MC will be in attendance', as were 'several bands of music'. Those wishing to take part in the picnic were asked to study the bills issued by the Blyth and Tyne Railway for the times of the trains.

In 1935 Mr E. Jarvis Garner of Nuneaton was secretary and commercial manager of the Pooley Hall Colliery, Polesworth near Tamworth, which at that time employed about 1,000 men. The pit was closed in the 1960s. Mr Garner organised an outing that year to the Aldershot Tattoo by train, the fare costing 5s, lunch and supper on the train 2s each, a reserved seat at the Tattoo, 7s 6d and another shilling for contingencies, the whole amounting to 18s 6d. It was agreed that there were to be no 'perks'—the usual free promotor's ticket—and any other benefits were to be paid for.

The co-operation of the local union, the directors of the colliery and the wages staff were sought, and it was agreed that those wishing to go could pay at the rate of 2s per ticket per week, the sum to be deducted from pay. There were 430 applicants for the outing—colliery workers and wives and friends.

On the day, the train left at 12.15, arriving at Fleet at about 4.30 p.m. Then a two-mile walk to the Rushmore Arena where the Tattoo was held. ('Being forty years ago, the weather was always fine, and this day was no exception,' recollects Mr Garner.)

The only cloud on the horizon was when the restaurant car conductor told Mr Garner that the party had drunk more bottled beer than had been anticipated and that there would not be enough for the return journey. Mr Garner's reply was to the point, 'These lads are miners, not Band of Hope boys. You have got nearly eight hours before we leave. You bloody well get plenty for the return journey, or else—.'

The Tattoo was a magnificent spectacle which all the party enjoyed. Another two-mile walk back to the train at Fleet and the journey home started—with plenty of bottled beer aboard! The profit of £22 on the outing went to a local hospital.

The *Ashington Collieries Magazine* of June 1926, which was the journal of the Ashington, Woodham, Linton and Ellington Collieries, reports an outing to London on Friday, 25 April of that year to see the Cup Final at Wembley on the following day. They left Ashington on the Friday at 10 p.m., arriving at King's Cross at 6.30 a.m. the next day. Breakfast was served at Slater's in Cheapside, where they went by charabanc, and a tour of London followed under the auspices of Thomas Cook. One miner startled the guide by asking, 'Wheor's Baker Street for Sexton Blake?' and when passing through the Billingsgate Fish market there was a brisk exchange of banter between those in the charabanc and the men working in the market. At Wembley they had reserved seats in the stadium, but the party was 'not particularly interested in either of the contesting teams'.

More poignant was an outing organised during the coal strike of 1926, when 124 miners decided to go on foot to Druridge Bay. Pit boots and shoes were hauled from their resting places where they had lain for eight weeks. It was a twenty-mile walk, there and back. The participants formed fours, and headed by banner bearers and Millburn's Band marched off with the tea-boiler and other equipment bringing up the rear. Soon they were on the main road to Ellington, where they caused a traffic hold-up, much to the annoyance of motorists, but the miners just smiled and went cheerfully on their way.

At Druridge Farm there was a halt for tea. Sticks were gathered, a fire lit and the contents of haversacks, bags and parcels were attacked by the hungry marchers. At Druridge, motor speed contests were taking place on the sands and a number of vehicles became embedded. The miners helped to haul them out, and grateful owners offered money, but it was refused. The marchers left Druridge just after ten at night, and in an hour and a half were home again, tired but satisfied.

The suburban garden, diligently cultivated between the wars, was to become the battleground in later years for industry to launch a campaign urging people to buy seeds, fertilisers and mechanical aids, but back in 1936 enthusiasts went on garden excursions by train to view the floral arrangements of some 224 stations which had entered the Railway's Gardening Competition. A train left Newcastle at noon on 23 August with 200 passengers for Kelso, permitting stops of fifteen minutes at Stannington, Warkworth, Longhoughton, Newhan, Velvet Hall and Sprouston for the excursionists to admire the gardens so lovingly tended by the staff who devoted time and money on bringing them to perfection. There was genuine pride in what had been achieved and much admiration expressed for the efforts made. Similar excursions, of 600 people, were organised from Middlesbrough to Hawes, Hull to Whitby, and Scarborough and York to Bridlington.

8

By Charabanc Between the Wars

'char-à-banc is a word still in popular use, in spite of the competition of *motor-coach* the spelling *charabanc* (plural *-s*) and pronunciation *sharabang* should be accepted . . .'
                    Fowler's *Modern English Usage*, Second Edition

Although the petrol-engined road vehicle was an uncertain starter in the years before the Great War, the military application of motor transport during the war itself had proved reliable and efficient. The Bristol Omnibus Company, for example, introduced the first charabanc in 1907, and by 1909 the company was advertising public tours by charabanc as far as Clevedon, Weston-super-Mare, Wells and Cheddar. At that time the speed limit was 12 m.p.h. and one of the drivers recollects being chased along the Hotwells Road by a policeman on a motorcycle and subsequently being charged with travelling at 14 m.p.h. Ironically the driver of a tram which overtook him at the time of the offence was unpunished as trams were subject to separate legislation!

In 1920 the charabanc was a 28-seater with solid tyres, and each individual row of seats had its own entrance door. A ladder was part of the standard equipment and passengers using the seats at the back needed to be reasonably agile. Pneumatic tyres were introduced in 1924 but the basic design of the vehicle itself did not change much until the 1930s.

Adjusting to life after the war was not easy. Lloyd George's promise to make Britain 'a fit country to live in' was not fulfilled, and in the attempt the face of Britain underwent major surgery in the form of ribbon development. In an earlier chapter there is a description of an outing when those taking part arrived at Pinner and strolled through some of the finest country in Middlesex to Eastcote. That was in 1909. In the 1930s the area was well on the way to being built up.

Henry Ford's Tin Lizzie, the bull-nose Morris Cowley and the Austin Seven (costing £165)—these pioneers of motoring were available for those who could afford to pay. Although houses were not always built with garages, there was often 'garage space'. Transport by road was becoming an acceptable way of life, and this was reflected in the preference for the charabanc over the train. The charabanc, hired for the day, belonged to you for that period of time. It was waiting for you when you wanted it. As was pointed out by Pratt and Pearce of Eastbourne in their Little Vic Orange Coach Tours brochure, 'You can stop where you like to admire the scenery or call for refreshment—you cannot do this when travelling by rail.' The charabanc was a sociable vehicle— your companions were round about you—and the driver might become a personal friend by the end of the day as a whip-round for his tip testified.

The comparatively uncluttered roads enabled the groups of people to go on half-day trips to the sporting fixtures, the seaside and places of interest. Shopping, cinema and theatre expeditions were simplified and service was door to door. In the first chapter, it may be remembered, those going by train to the Epsom Races in 1838 had to make their own way on foot from Kingston to Epsom. Some eighty years later an Orange Luxury Coach would have taken them 'right on the rails' for £1, and the Derby could have been watched without leaving the vehicle.

Restrictions on pleasure trips, necessary because of the war, were removed on 2 January 1919, but before the engines were started up again that summer, it seems appropriate to record an outing of almost Victorian tranquillity that took place in May of that year when a party of girls from the Toilet Department of Christopher Thomas & Brothers Ltd went on a Saturday afternoon,

'rambling to Combe Dingle. Boarding the tramcar at the Centre [of Bristol], we arrived at Durdham Down at 2.45 p.m. We walked over the Downs, then along country lanes, noting the beautiful scenes of nature. We rambled beyond the tea gardens at Combe Dingle along the road to the wood, where we sat and rested, being tired after a long walk. Here snapshot photographs were taken, which caused much fun, as we were all unprepared. Leaving the woods we strolled through some fields, and about 5 p.m. we made our way to the Rose Cottage Tea Rooms where we did full justice to a splendid tea (even to the last remains of the jam!) . . . The return journey was made through the fields, reaching the car terminus at Westbury about 7.17 p.m.'

One of the more amusing sights of the 1920s and 1930s was to see a charabanc parked by the kerb at a seaside resort containing a party of excursionists bound for a 'mystery' tour. Those already in the vehicle looked slightly embarrassed as passers-by made appropriate remarks and smiled indulgently. The board propped against the charabanc announced in decorative letters SELECTED 'MYSTERY TOUR' TO ???. Murray & Sons, who ran such tours from Stranraer, were quite eloquent about it:

'Who has not read and enjoyed a mystery thriller? Surely no person with a love of adventure, suspense and romance . . . Leaving Stranraer patrons of these tours will be in the dark to their ultimate destination, and the "mystery" deepens as the coach speeds merrily past woodland, dale, pasture fields, and by the silvery sea, all sorts of conjectures will be made as to the route which will next be taken . . . We are at liberty to say that many side and unclassified roads will be covered, and passengers will —not that they will cavil at the suggestion—be lost for a little time among the wilds of Grey Galloway.'

The tours left Stranraer at 2.30 p.m. and 7 p.m. and the fares were 1s 6d, 2s 6d and 3s 6d.

Fleet Cars Ltd, Torquay and Paignton, which had 'all cars fitted with the latest type of Pneumatic Equipment and most modern methods of springing in order to obtain perfect resiliency', organised a tour penetrating the history of the west country in the tradition of Drake and Raleigh who set sail not always knowing where they were going. It was known as a 'Sealed Orders' tour, which might be 'of the sea or the moors, the hill tops or the valleys. We do not know; the driver does not know. He and you are sailing under sealed orders. A thousand years of romance are calling.'

Descriptions of other tours in the company's guide were specially written by Dr L. Du Garde Peach, author of *Unknown Devon*. In between the wars, on the first Wednesday after the Summer Sale, Bentalls of Worthing closed shop at midday and the staff went on a 'mystery tour' outing in Southdown coaches.

Mystery tours in the evening had an additional thrill and Lowland Motorways ran these from Glasgow. For the working man and and his family it was pleasant after a hard day's work to be taken away from the city to an unknown destination, even if it was recognisable when you reached it. Evening tours from seaside resorts were popular. To go forth with a loved one to an unknown destination, the moon shining and the stars twinkling, was a romantic experience.

The coach companies made the fullest use of their mobility to attract the custom of particular groups of people who might benefit from an excursion to a particular place for a specific purpose. After a day's shopping or whatever, it was rather a drab ending to an enjoyable day just to return home in time to cook the old man's supper. A play, cinema or music hall was needed to round off the day, the cost of the seat being sometimes included in the fare.

Wright Brothers (Burnley) Ltd in about 1927 appealed to 'Shop Assistants and other Business People' to visit Leeds—'the acknowledged GREATEST AND BEST SHOPPING CENTRE IN THE NORTH OF ENGLAND'. Pullman Saloon service was advertised to the Leeds Pantomime and patrons arrived in good time to look round the city 'and afterwards to enjoy a comfortable seat in the Orchestra Stalls at the Theatre'. The inclusive fare was 14s 6d and light refreshments were supplied at no extra charge on the return journey.

In October 1924 the National Omnibus & Transport Company Ltd of Colchester advertised a Theatre Coach—a special fourteen-seater saloon bus—leaving the Town Hall at 2 p.m. for the Alhambra Theatre, London. The performance began at 6.10 p.m., finished at 8.25 and the party returned to Colchester at nine o'clock. The return fare, which included a numbered and reserved seat in the front row of the dress circle, was 10s 6d. A particular feature of the outing was the wireless concert in the coach *en route* there and back.

In 1926 United Automobile Services Ltd, Darlington, ran Pantomime Buses to the Empire Theatre, Newcastle, to see 'Jack and Jill' with George Formby of ukelele fame as Jack. The return fare, including a Royal Stall ticket was 13s 6d (11s 6d for a seat in the Orchestra Stalls) and the company would reserve tables at Perry's High Class Restaurant, which boasted a 'London Orchestra' (at an inclusive price of 19s 6d and 16s 6d respectively).

Although the popularity of the motor coach was evident, the more sedate and old-fashioned forms of transport appealed when the area covered was limited and not efficiently served by roads. E. Nelson, the Garage and Livery Stables, Arnside, Westmorland, advertised landaulettes and victorias as being available at any time for tours of the Eight Lakes. The year is not specified on the leaflet, but it is likely to be pre-1930, as swastikas formed the border decoration on the printed matter.

Bartlett's of Shanklin in the Isle of Wight organised afternoon excursions by the four-horse ('Old Times') and pair-horse ('The Times') coaches. Trips were made to Sea View and St Helens for 4s; also to Arreton, Ashey Down, Nunwell Park and Brading; Wroxall, Top of the Undercliff, Whitwell and Godshill. Bath chairs were available for invalids, and brakes, wagonettes, landaus, victorias, dog carts, broughams, etc., could be hired. Private motor coaches and charabancs—if anybody needed them—could be hired by arrangement.

If there was competition between road and rail, there was also competition between the coach companies. Each set out to pamper their patrons, as they were called, with greater comfort due to pneumatic tyres, spring seats, travelling rugs, and illustrated guides with maps which described in detail the places visited.

Yellow Motor Coaches (Folkestone Motors Ltd) advertised that their 'easy and quiet-running Coaches are the smartest and most Up-to-Date in Folkestone; fitted with Cape Cart Hood for showery weather. Construction of body entirely protects passengers from the usual Dust Nuisance'.

Embankment Cars, Plymouth, which toured in Devon and Cornwall were not only the last word in road comfort and convenience, 'they are in the hands of experienced drivers—a rather important feature of Devon and Cornwall' in view of the treacherous going.

The Yorkshire Woollen District Transport Co. Ltd, in 1938 offered Holiday Coupons at 3s 6d and 1s which provided for a holiday journey or a day's outing, but if the purchaser was, for any reason, unable to make use of his coupons the face value was refunded.

In 1926 The United Automobile Services Ltd issued photographic views of the beauty spots covered by their tours. Views of Blackhall Rocks, Collywell Bay, Gainford Village, Seaton Sluice Harbour, Newbiggin Bay, etc. were printed on cards bearing, in the top left-hand corner The United Automobile Services logo, and in the right-hand bottom corner were the words 'taken with a "Kodak" '. Kodak cameras were given away:

'No holidaymaker should be without a Camera to provide real and lasting memory of happy days. By arrangement with Kodak Ltd., we are therefore pleased to announce we shall give away No. 2 Cartridge Model "C" Hawk-Eye Cameras to passengers by "United Yellow" Motor Coach Tours.'

Passengers needed to collect the counterfoils of ten advance booking tickets to qualify.

The Shamrock and Rambler Motor Coaches Ltd, Bournemouth which ran day tours to Cheddar Gorge, Caves and Wells Cathedral for 12s 6d, and elsewhere offered to refund money 'in case of inclement weather'. Furthermore, by leaving an address, a car would be sent, without fee, to collect you from where you were staying. The brochure also announced that at W. H. Smith, The Square, Bournemouth, there was 'delightful music each morning and afternoon', the orchestra and first-class artistes being under the direction of Mr F. G. Bacon.

Coach passengers today on a sightseeing tour are kept informed about places of interest by a guide who gives a running commentary through a microphone. Such sophistication was not available between the wars. Patrons of Greenslades Tours, Exeter, were handed a guide on entering the charabanc in which the most important items of interest on the tour were numbered. On arriving at each numbered item the driver attracted the attention of passengers by pressing an electric bell, and by referring to the numbered item in the guide it was possible to read an account of the place in view. As the brochure pointed out, this 'Silent Guide' eliminated the danger which used to arise when a driver turned round to explain the historical interest of a particular building or scene.

Variations of this idea were used by Southdown and other coach firms, and a company was formed called The Silent Guide Patented Service of 82 Victoria Street, London, S.W.1 which supplied appropriate guides to coach firms in different parts of the country. The trade names of the guides was Scenaidicator under the editorship of Charles G. Harper, 'the Historian of the British Highways'. Instead of an electric bell a gong was sounded when the number was reached.

There were few important race meetings all over the country that were not covered by the coach firms, and the fares were highly competitive. Racegoers in 1922 who booked with The London Provincial Motor Touring Service of Upper Baker Street, London could attend the City and Suburban for an inclusive price of 30s per head to cover the fare, parking on the rails near the grand stand, a sandwich-and-champagne luncheon, and tea and dinner at the Holborn Restaurant. For Ascot, to include lunch and tea at the Royal Hotel, the charge was 21s. Goodwood cost 27s 6d to include a 'first-class' lunch and tea. General Country Services of Reigate, Surrey, in 1932 charged 5s return from Redhill to Epsom to see the Derby, the fare to include admission to the Private Enclosure near Tattenham Corner, 'where a splendid view of racing can be obtained'.

An incident is recorded in the *Carrow Works Magazine* in 1923 when the Staff and Departmental Managers of Colman's, Norwich, visited Ipswich and Norwich. Charabancs took the party through the Constable country, but the drivers appeared to be strangers to the locality. At every junction in the road there was some speculation as to where the leading vehicle had gone. One driver, who appeared to be pouring a stream of information about the locality into the ears of the ladies beside him was, in fact, giving authoritative tips 'straight from the horse's mouth' about the runners in the Derby taking place the following day.

It was in the 1930s, when unemployment rose to $2\frac{1}{2}$ million as a result of the depression, Hitler and Mussolini ranted, raved and invaded, Mosley's black-shirted British Union of Fascists created diversions mainly in the east end of London, the Spanish Civil War provided a rehearsal for the World War that was to come,

K

Chamberlain promised peace in our time, and Edward VIII abdicated, that the British people were being trundled round Britain in charabancs which penetrated every corner. Crowding into cathedrals and cafés, seeking sun and sea, the search was for relaxation and a chance to turn away from the ever-recurring crises. Coach tours were of seven days' duration or longer, and extended to the Continent, although business did suffer in the slump of the early 1930s.

Whatever the occasion there was a charabanc to take you to it. Lewis of Greenwich sent coach parties on visits to the Stately Homes of England. Longleat (taking in Stonehenge) cost 12s 6d return. For the same price a day at Beaulieu was possible which took in Lyndhurst. United Service Transport Co. Ltd of Clapham would, in 1933, take you to Whipsnade Zoo and back for 5s. Orange Luxury coaches, London, conveyed those wanting to see the Aldershot Coronation Tattoo for the sum of 8s 6d to 16s inclusive of ticket and depending on the day. Eight hours in Blackpool, gaping at the illuminations, was in 1938 enjoyed by those living in Birmingham and district at a cost of 12s 6d paid to Midland Red, which took them there and back. In 1932 General Country Services from Redhill advertised excursions to South-ampton for 8s return to view the White Star Liners which at that time had regular scheduled journeys across the Atlantic.

In the 1930s, from May to September, George Ewer (and others) ran tours in their Grey-Green Coaches of the hopfields in Kent, picking up passengers from Enfield, Edmonton, Tottenham, Stamford Hill, Mildmay Park, Dalston, Shoreditch, Mile End, Hackney, Clapton and Leyton for 4s, increased to 5s at week-ends and bank holidays.

The public houses and hotels on the main charabanc routes catered for the thousands of trippers who stopped on the way to their destinations. Although welcomed for the money they spent, they were not always welcomed for their behaviour.

A party would arrive and, like locusts, descend on a public house. As suddenly as they had arrived the locusts left, leaving behind a legacy of dirty glasses, spilled beer, insanitary lavatories and stubbed cigarette-ends on the floor of the bar. No wonder that some regulars cringed in horror at such invasions and with-drew to quieter places where the pint could be enjoyed in peace.

So the publican had to make up his mind. If he was to cater for charabanc parties he had to go all out for the business, come to an arrangement with the coach companies and drivers to ensure that his pub was a stopping place, extend his premises so that parties could be catered for, supply parking space for the charabancs, employ extra staff—in short, extend a welcome. Other publicans put up notices NO COACHES and withdrew, valuing the steady custom of regulars and occasional visitors to the seasonal trade of the coach parties.

On the whole, standards of catering at places *en route* were satisfactory, although Mr C. Squires of Harrogate, who worked for a firm of high-class caterers and provision merchants in Hull, remembers that in 1929, when his firm went to Scarborough on an outing, the party stopped at an hotel for a three-course lunch of soup, roast lamb and mint sauce, peas, new potatoes, sweet and coffee. Being of Yorkshire blood and employed by high-class caterers the meal was considered unsatisfactory, and the manager was told in no uncertain terms what the party thought of the watered soup and tough old lamb.

When Allied Paper Merchants (Wiggins Teape & Co.) Ltd wanted to go on an outing in June 1939, they were quoted by the West Yorkshire Road Car Co. Ltd of East Parade, Harrogate, the sum of £10 return for supplying a 32-seater coach to be at the Allied Paper Merchants' Albion Street, Leeds address at 7.15 a.m. for a journey to Blackpool. Arrangements were made for stops to be made at Guisburn and Stanley Park, Blackpool (where sporting events were to be held by kind permission of the Blackpool Corporation).

Lunch was served at the County Hotel, Central Promenade and the menu consisted of green pea soup; fried fillets of plaice, tartare sauce; roast lamb, mint sauce or cold meats and salads; cabbage, green peas, baked or boiled potatoes; fruit tart and cream, rice pudding; cheese and biscuits. The cost worked out at about 3s per head.

Blackpool was always a popular centre for a day's outing. No. 1 Stamping Department of Lever Bros, Port Sunlight, went there in August 1923. 'Weather, grand! Spirits high! Photographer, smiling!' it was recorded in *Port Sunlight News* of August of that year. A party of 190 in seven charabancs started from Pier Head at 7.30 a.m. and then took the route Ormskirk, Langton, Preston. A break for about twenty minutes was made at Langton for 'light refreshments and jazz'. Soon after arriving at Blackpool at eleven o'clock there was lunch. Instructions were given, 'Do as you like, go where you like, but do enjoy yourselves.' In consequence Blackpool was explored, although some did not move from the sunny sands. At 7.45 p.m. the charabancs began the return journey.

Every effort was made by the seaside resorts to attract this new public of day visitors. Coach parking facilities near the sea front were necessary and even more important was the provision of indoor entertainment when the weather was bad. A day outing, longed for and saved up for, could be ruined by bad weather and the resorts which supplied alternative entertainment reaped the harvest. As the crowds drifted along the promenade and sampled the amusement arcades and the gift shops, there was ample opportunity for the visitors to return home without much more than a penny in purse or pocket. The municipal authorities had spent many thousands of pounds in making their resorts attractive for all conditions of climate, and it was reasonable that they should be rewarded financially by levying higher rates, profiting from municipal undertakings ranging from deck chairs to entertainment on the pier, and seeking the best return from commercial firms renting space in important and strategic parts of the town and seafront.

'I am very pleased to hear that Scarborough has been selected for your Outing this year. I sincerely hope that your visit will be in every way an interesting and pleasant one, and that you will take away with you many happy recollections of your visit to the "Queen of the Watering Places".'

So wrote William Boyes, Mayor of Scarborough in the Illustrated Souvenir Programme on the occasion of the outing of the Managers of the London and North Eastern Railway, W. H. Smith bookstalls and other relevant departments, accompanied by their wives. Understandably the party travelled by train to Scarborough station on 9 June 1925, where they arrived at 11.30. Messrs Robinson's fleet of motor coaches collected them for a tour of Scarborough and environments. Visits were paid to Alexandra Gardens and Peasholm Lake and Park. They toured

North Bay, Marine Drive, South Foreshore, Ramsdale Valley, Esplanade, Rose Gardens and the Italian Gardens. All these places were described in the souvenir programme by Mr R. A. H. Goodyear, author of boys' books of school life and adventure, who lived in the neighbourhood. At 12.15 a photograph was taken of the party by a member of the firm's Scarborough printing works. Back in the coaches for the tour to continue to Oliver's Mount, where a wreath was placed on the War Memorial which bore the names of three employees of W. H. Smith who had been killed in action during the Great War. Lunch at the Grand Hotel consisting of cold salmon, roast lamb, peach melba with all the appropriate trimmings, and later there was room for a tea of egg-and-cress sandwiches, brown bread and butter, preserves, fancy cakes, pastries.

The firm presented the ladies with a box of chocolates and the men were handed cigars. A nice touch was that when the party left Scarborough Station to return home, the station master, by way of a spirited farewell, put detonators on the line which went off as the train left the station, which prompted one of the London visitors to remark that he always thought things went off well in the north, but did not realise that they went off with a bang.

A house journal description of an outing tends to include a number of 'in' jokes and references incomprehensible to outsiders and therefore all the more to be encouraged by those 'in the know'. Pilkington Bros house journal, *Cullet*, of October 1936 gives an account of the Plate Works Glass Bevellers' ('Revellers for the day') annual outing to Morecambe and Blackpool on Saturday, 4 July 1936.

The writer recalls the days of the one- and two-horse wagonette in which the bevellers were conveyed to a little pub 'that provided the rabbit pie "do", and with bowls of juicy gravy that the old brigade used to sup out of so as not to waste time and to be in time "fur't me'at" '. In 1936 it was the 32-seater de luxe charabanc which conveyed the bevellers to their destination, due to start at 9 o'clock but delayed appropriately by the latest newly-weds for whom plenty of excuses were made. Never, it was pointed out, had the outing ever had to be postponed because of bad weather. Organisers were advised to select the first Saturday in July if they wanted 'Bevellers' Weather'.

After calls on the way for 'Bottles of Pop' a good dinner was eaten at Morecambe, and after a stroll and a thirst-quencher the party left for Blackpool in time for tea.

'Then the fun began. We spread out: some went to watch the four "Jack Charnocks" show their skill . . . some for donkey and pony rides; and others shopping. And what shoppers. Baby dolls, Stuffed Bunnies and Teddies, to say nothing of Rattles . . . What proud fathers, and how bashful! It was a treat to see how they smuggled all their treasures into the Charas. Ask Dicky Booth! The way he led his army of young "marrieds" up was a treat . . . Anyhow, 11.30 was ever even late enough for the Bevellers, and we left for home to the accompaniment of the loud speaker, all tired and happy. And what's that? How many Drunks? None: but it would not be a Bevellers' outing if it was a teetotal "do". Anyhow we could all sing "The King" and be understood when we parted at 1.15 a.m. A fine day and a happy family . . . Looking forward to the next time and thanking the Firm for the time off.'

A correspondent recollects the period 1924 to about 1935 when her mother, a Sunday School Superintendent, organised an annual outing to the sea from a South Yorkshire mining village to Cleethorpes or possibly Skegness. The charabanc conveying them had a convertible roof, and when the weather was fine it was rolled back so that the health-giving ozone could be absorbed to the fullest. The cost of the outing was 2s 6d for children, 5s for adults and contributions of a penny a week were begun directly after Christmas.

'Are you going?' That was the question asked weeks before the Great Day. The worst disaster that could happen was to get some childish ailment and have to miss the occasion. The cost included a free packed lunch which miraculously appeared from a wicker clothes basket on arriving at the sandy beach. Each child brought his or her own bottle of lemonade to quench a glorious thirst. A wonderful eight hours was spent on the sandy beach paddling, playing cricket and riding on the donkeys. Children with more money could afford the roundabouts.

Leaving the beach was heartbreaking, but at 7 p.m. the party gathered to board the charabanc for the homeward journey to the accompaniment of happy songs and hymns. On one occasion a ten-year-old girl failed to arrive for the homeward journey and the charabanc left without her. The mother who had organised the outing had to remain at the police station while they searched for her. Eventually she was found, so overcome and fascinated by the whole scene that she had lost all account of time. She returned home by the mail train the following morning.

A booze-up was an accepted tradition of a charabanc outing. Only the driver needed to remain sober. The vehicle itself was well stacked with bottles of beer, and there were frequent stops at public houses *en route*. This was not possible if the party went by train. There is little doubt that women interfered with a good booze-up and there was a tendency for all-male or all-women outings. A 'mixed' outing was inhibiting for those intent upon drinking. For many employees the prospect of uninhibited drinking was the only reason for the outing. The weather was of little consequence; in fact a wet day encouraged drinking because there was little else to do. There is a poem in the *Kodak Works Bulletin*, July 1921, which points to a trend of thought:

> The 'sharrys' were pretty well loaded,
> And you should have heard the boys cheer
> When they spotted the Committee stowing
> The 'vittles' and 'shush', bottled beer!
>
> Soon on the road we were moving
> And passed through old Watford at nine
> But we didn't see nary a native,
> P'raps because it was not opening time.
>
> But though we pulled up good and plenty,
> And had several drinks on the way,
> There wasn't a man too much sir,
> And everyone had a good day.

Although it was claimed that nobody ever got objectionably drunk, the public houses on the main coast roads at ten o'clock at night were often frequented by beery, belching individuals, red of face, noisy and unsteady as they clambered back into their coaches for the homeward journey, the hiccups and the bawdy songs floating outwards into the warm night air.

Music was an integral part of the enjoyment. Mouth organs, combs over which lavatory paper (the thin variety unlike the rough stuff in use to-day) was placed, swanee whistles, the banjo or ukelele—instruments that could be carried easily or slipped into a pocket—were produced once the charabanc had started. A popular tune was played diffidently at first. Then someone would begin singing and soon the whole coach could be heard joining in the chorus. An accordion or squeeze-box, a more ambitious instrument, was also popular. On the way home the instrument-playing became more confused—drink does not always assist wind-playing—and the voices, loud and not always very clear, took over.

It was the age of jazz, and on arrival at a public house there was invariably a piano and possibly drums and percussion, although if there were not they were sometimes brought by the party who had managed to get them loaded on to the coach.

Robinson's White Lounge Coaches, whose excursion area included Flamborough and Bridlington, Hemsley and Rievaulx Abbey, carried this advertisement in their brochure:

A Day's Outing is incomplete without the WRIGHT Songs.
The 1925 Song-Dance Hits include:
'Shanghai'; 'Oh, How I love my Darling'; 'Close in
My Arms'; 'Toy Drum Major'
Lawrence Wright Music Company

Workers went for their firms' outings to the coast and elsewhere, but there was a considerable amount of traffic taking people to see firms at work. In 1938 and 1939 Southdown Motor Services' Special Attraction was a visit to 'the Glorious West Country' from Brighton, to include Fry's Chocolate Works, Keynsham and Model Village, Somerdale. 'A generous sample of Fry's Products is presented to each passenger on leaving.' The return fare was £1, which included tea and a conducted tour of the works.

The same coach company gave excursionists an opportunity to see over the works of Morris Motors, Cowley, 'or visit Oxford' . . . 'the City of Domes and Spires'. A description of what the visitor would see at Cowley makes interesting reading in the light of working conditions in the motor industry to-day:

'. . . Thousands of men are working—thousands of cars are taking shape. From the various specialized Morris factories, the parts arrive at Cowley continuously. Engines . . . bodies . . . wings . . . axles . . . chassis frames . . . radiators . . . wheels—a constant stream is arriving, to be instantly sorted out for assembly. Then as the chassis frames move slowly along the conveyors, various parts are assembled at different points along the line. Everything happens with clockwork precision. Men and machines are synchronised. From out of a maze of separate parts, complete cars emerge. They grow before your eyes. It is a spectacle worth travelling hundreds of miles to see; a symbol of modernity and progress; an experience you will value all your life.'

The return fare from Brighton (including tea) was 15s 6d, but if you only visited Oxford, 6d less and no tea.

Within a short time the works at Cowley were engaged in the manufacture of more lethal weapons than motor cars. Fry's products were hard to come by. The coaches that carried civilians were put to other uses. When once it had been possible to select a place for an outing or excursion, now one was conveyed compulsorily to a place one had no particular desire to visit. The signposts on the road were removed, and in the best tradition of the 'mystery tour' of more stable days, people sometimes had difficulty in knowing where they were.

And nearly forty years later that could still be said to apply.

9

Exit the Day Outing, Enter the Package Holiday

' "Now! Now!" cried the Queen. "Faster! Faster!" and they went
so fast that at last they seemed to skim through the air, hardly
touching the ground with their feet.'
Through the Looking Glass by Lewis Carroll

The title of this chapter is not, of course, strictly accurate. The
day outing still exists but attitudes towards it differ from those
taken up to the outbreak of the Second World War, and the world
is a different place. 'Mystery' tours do still exist at seaside resorts,
railway enthusiasts haul steam locomotives from railway museums
and travel on lines infrequently used, firms continue to arrange
annual outings (and those who do not have substituted dinners
and similar functions), but it is a shadow of what was done up
up to the Second World War. Affluence, the motor car, the welfare
state, management/worker relationship, women at work, have all
diminished the importance of an outing. People gather together
for a specific purpose—convenience, cheapness and because by
so doing they *profit* by it; an excursion to a town, perhaps,
because the shops there offer better value. This was also true
of the period covered by this book but then pleasure was also
taken into account. Today the impression prevails that people
want to get home quickly because time cannot be spared for
frivolities. As W. H. Davies wrote:

What is this life if, full of care,
We have no time to stand and stare?

An outing for a day was, at one period of history, a 'holiday'.
And yet in 1975 it was estimated that about eight million people

went without a holiday because they were too old, infirm, disabled, or on fixed incomes which failed to take account of inflation. The organisations that, in Victorian times, would have arranged a day outing for such people now organise at least a week at the seaside or country. To-day, local authorities subsidise such holidays, but those taking them generally contribute a sum of money weekly. On 24 August 1975 the *Sunday Times* reported how a family of man, wife, daughter, two sons and baby grandson spent a week at the seaside for the £52 they had contributed, the true cost being in the region of £115. For that they ate meat twice in the week, watched colour television in the lounge and had rooms with hot and cold running water. So, through the rates, the whole community contributes toward giving real holidays to those who are unable to afford one at current prices.

In Victorian times the day outing was the best that some charitable organisations could achieve in the way of a holiday for the poor they helped, although in many instances longer periods away were arranged at holiday homes built or rented for the purpose. The private benefactor was much in evidence and so were the people who needed help. To-day, poverty tends to be hidden behind the curtains and has to be discovered.

The available means of transport were limited in Victorian times to the horse-drawn waggon, boat, train, and the travellers' legs, of which considerable use were made. Until the arrival of the charabanc excursionists were deposited by train at a particular point, and to reach the sea, green fields, a race meeting or similar event it was necessary to walk considerable distances in some cases. The distance that could be covered by a horse-drawn vehicle was limited and passengers needed to jump off the waggon at steep hills and help the horses on their way. It was part of the fun and as one correspondent recollects such hardships were cheerfully tolerated. The Sunday School outing to Pevensey Bay was anticipated with great excitement, and the arrival of horses looking so smart with their shining brasses and little bells on the harness ringing at every movement added to the pleasure. Pocket money had been diligently saved so that a stick of rock might be purchased as evidence that the sea had been reached.

In the minutes of the Stafford Photographic Society it was recorded that in 1907 a summer's day outing took place during which 'the lower road between Alton and Oakemoor was traversed and the scenery much photographed'. Pasted on a page of the Society's minutes is a photograph of a group of eight gentlemen and two ladies resting from the toils of carrying their cumbersome photographic equipment about with them on foot.

It was the railways that really opened up the country by collecting people from the small wayside halts to take them to the sea that many of them had lived near but had not seen. Having discovered the sea there was the desire to go on it, but the sea could not have been reached at all had it not been for the railways.

The charabanc, between the wars, challenged the railways and a fierce battle for the excursion market ensued. Motorised transport could convey people to even more remote places which the railways could not reach. A combined rail and charabanc outing was a popular possibility because on arriving at a station there was a charabanc to convey excursionists on a sight-seeing tour. There was no need to walk unless you were a dedicated hiker, in which case the main railway stations were a starting point for the countryside with its fields and paths. A 'Mystery Express' took hikers, unaware of their destination, out in the country and let them hike for some hours before rejoining the train for home. A moonlight walk over the Sussex Downs to see the sun rise from Chanctonbury Ring was another popular outing. A dedicated hiker was one thing; but if it was possible to ride everywhere there were many people anxious to take advantage of it. The introduction of cheap day returns on the railways enabled families to travel on the Southern (for example) from Victoria to the Surrey hills, and it was standing room only for those who tried to join the train *en route* on a summer Sunday morning.

The private car did more than anything else to kill the old-fashioned conception of an outing. The organised outing lost its appeal. The realisation by the car owner that he could go anywhere at a moment's notice without planning ahead was a revolutionary situation. The private motorist—a trickle of them between the wars—flooded the roads after the Second World War. Lack of good roads constrained his freedom until motorways gave him back that freedom. But once off the motorway the secondary routes were choked with traffic and the massive charabanc—now known as a coach—in which his ancestors had travelled with such pleasure was an obstacle which prevented him reaching his destination within a reasonable time.

The railways, now nationalised, and having to compete with the road and air travel, drastically cut access to the regions that were unprofitable. The halts and wayside stations where the gardens had been admired by excursionists in the 1930s were now overgrown. Grass and weeds covered the track over which at one time fussy little steam engines pulled carriages filled with happy passengers on a day outing.

Air travel was the key to travel abroad. Now at last, it was possible to visit countries bathed, it seemed, in perpetual sunshine at a considerably lower cost than a holiday of similar duration in Britain, where fine weather was not assured. The holiday season— late July to early September—when everyone seemed to be away meant that in Britain the roads were overcrowded, accommodation had to be booked far in advance and the bill at the end of a stay in an hotel or boarding house was sometimes out of all proportion to the value given. The aeroplane, like some magic carpet, conveyed the holidaymaker to sunshine and freedom away from the enclosed island in which he spent most of his days.

Holidays with pay, generous overtime and full employment ensured that money to pay for a holiday abroad was no problem. The holidaymaker may have fled from his own country to avoid its confines, but his compatriots followed in his wake and by cocking an ear there were the different dialects he would have heard had he been at Blackpool, Clacton or Southend. In fact the presence of so many countrymen was reassuring. There was little or no attempt to learn the language of the country visited because English in varying dialects would be heard everywhere, and it was worth while hoteliers coming to terms with the British way of feeding and drinking so that the visitors should feel 'at home'.

In the light of extended holidays with pay, varied and quick methods of transport and inflation the concept of the 'outing' has changed. Whereas in the past an outing was an occasion, now it is a pleasant diversion. Only those devoid of transport to get about or those confined to their homes for some reason look upon the annual outing in the same light as they might have done in their youth. The family business with its handful of employees has not survived the economic storms of the times. It has been absorbed into large, impersonal organisations in which there are clubs, enabling members to enjoy time spent abroad at a low cost made possible by the financial advantages of group travel.

On the notice boards appear announcements similar to this actual example:

A WEEK-END IN FANTASTIC PARIS

No passports required

Day 1 (Friday).
Depart Factory at 10 pm relaxing in the comfortable seats of our luxury coach we take the fast motorway journey to Dover for the short crossing to France.

Day 2 (Saturday). We arrive in France as dawn is breaking and drive through the morning (naturally stopping for a French coffee en route) to Paris and arrive at our centrally situated hotel at mid-day. Now all the afternoon free to see the sights of Europe's brightest capital ... The Eiffel Tower, Champs Elysées, pavement cafes, the 'Quartier Latin', a 'Bateau Mouche' ride on the Seine, Notre Dame, Sacré Coeur ...

A low priced optional evening excursion is available to see the wonderful lights of Paris.

Day 3 (Sunday). After breakfast a short time is free for last-minute shopping, then we wave good-bye to Paris and we're on our way home. We travel back through France and via Calais/ Dover to return home at approximately midnight.

Price includes: Coach transportation, Boat fare, 1 night's bed and breakfast accommodation, services of representative throughout.

COLOUR, ROMANCE, GAIETY—A TOUCH OF SPICE OF LIFE IN EUROPE'S SAUCIEST CAPITAL ...
Full duty free allowance.

No time off from work; no direct financial contribution from the firm, although quite what the quality of Monday's work is like remains to be seen. But such an excursion would not be possible unless the organisation was a large one and the firm was willing to provide facilities under which their employees could join clubs and benefit accordingly. Firms possibly contribute to a welfare fund that makes such excursions a reality, but it is the employees who determine how such welfare contributions shall be spent.

The traditional Englishman's idea of Paris as 'saucy' still exists in the late twentieth century. Now that excursions take place abroad it is appropriate to examine the Englishman's attitude towards foreign parts. The Continental moved with relative ease from one country to another. The Englishman, with some twenty-two miles of water separating him from 'abroad', had to overcome a formidable obstacle. In 1840 the total number of passengers passing through ports to Calais and Boulogne was 72,000; by 1860 it was 179,751, and by 1872 the figure was 273,081. By the mid-nineteenth century most of the short sea routes were in the hands of the railway companies. In 1836, before the railways reached the Channel, a single first-class fare from London to Calais was 28s. Some twenty-five years later, when the railways existed, the fare for the same distance was 30s. Easter week-end return tickets in 1848 from London to Boulogne cost 27s first class, 20s second class, and in 1850 the South Eastern Railway offered punters an opportunity to attend the races at Boulogne for 28s, 20s, 15s return, depending on the class of travel selected. In 1840 there were excursions from London to Paris from 44s return. All-inclusive tours abroad organised by travel agents were available—according to advertisements in *The Times*—in the 1840s. The railway companies considered their Dover and Folkestone services to be first-class routes, and those from Newhaven second class.

Between the wars there were cheap excursions to Paris and resorts along the north coast of France. To-day the hovercraft has lessened the time it takes to cross the Channel but seasonal traffic is something of a misnomer. Extensive forays in the winter months are made to shops in Calais and other French ports to stock up with duty-free drink at prices financially beneficial even allowing for the fares which can no longer be considered cheap. In return the French invade Marks and Spencer in England's south coast towns for clothes they can buy cheaper than in France. From as far afield as Norway the English east coast ports are frequented by those in search of bargains. But, as was implied at the beginning of this chapter, such expeditions are materialistic. Laden with legally acquired loot the excursionists return to their respective countries and pull up the drawbridges, so to speak.

When (or doubtless before) the last bottle is emptied, or the clothes show signs of wear and tear, then off they go again. Any fun there may be is incidental. Gain is the main consideration.

Crossing the Channel was generally unpleasant although, for those who could afford it, there was comfort to be had. As early as 1790 the passage to France from Brighthelmston (Brighton as we now know it) to Dieppe took place every Saturday evening. The vessel contained two 'elegant' cabins, eight beds in each, 'either of which can be taken separately'. Horses and carriages had to be sent the day before sailing, and it was pointed out that the route to London by way of Dieppe and Brighthelmston was ninety miles nearer than by way of Dover and Calais.

Every effort was made to overcome the scourge of seasickness. Lord Macaulay, in a letter from Paris in 1843, described his passage from Brighton to Dieppe.

'We had not got out of sight of the Beachy Head lights, when it began to rain hard. I was therefore driven to the cabin, and compelled to endure the spectacle, and to hear the unutterable groans and gasps, of fifty seasick people. I went out when the rain ceased; but everything on deck was now soaked. It was impossible to sit, so I walked up and down the vessel all night . . .'

Contemporary paintings of the nineteenth century show the abject misery of those on board cross-channel boats, huddled together against spray and wind, pale of face and probably with empty stomachs. It is sad to record the failure of Mr Bessemer's invention, a suspended saloon in a vessel, hydraulically operated, whereby, when the vessel moved from side to side, the saloon remained level. In 1875 a new steamship with the suspended saloon made the journey from Dover to Calais with 200 passengers on board. Initially there was mist and rain but it soon vanished. The sea was calm and the wind, too, was favourable, so there was little opportunity of proving how efficient the suspended saloon was. On entering Calais the vessel ran against one of the wooden piers. Admirable as the invention was, it was considered a failure.

And on arrival at Calais and Dieppe, what did the tourists find? There was no excuse if they had not come prepared. 'Annoyance to Tourists' stated an advertisement in the 1860s. 'How often a night's rest is disturbed by Insect Worries! If travellers will take

with them some of KEATINGS CELEBRATED INSECT POWDER
they can be freed from these annoyances.' But even if the bed was
free from bugs there was the danger of fire. Foreigners had little
respect for the danger inherent in wooden buildings, inadequate
fire precautions, narrow staircases. Merryweather advertised a
'Kit-Bag' Fire Escape (as supplied to H.H. the Khedive of Egypt),
and it was stressed that no visitor to hotels should be without such
a simple life-saving appliance, and £3 was a small price to pay for
safety and peace of mind.

It was common knowledge that foreigners paid scant attention
to sanitary conditions. ' "What a dreadful smell!" said the uniniti-
ated stranger, enveloping his nose in his pocket handkerchief. "It
is the smell of the Continent, sir," replied the man of experience.
As so it was.' Thus Mrs Frances Trollope in *Paris and the Parisians*, 1835. Sewage was there for all to see and smell, so there was a
certain sale for a metal pail, disguised as a bonnet box, with a
removable polished mahogany rim and metal lid, the possession
of which would save ladies from 'having to encounter, to meet and
glide by the moustached foreigner (be he noble or pedlar) with
his waistcoat unbuttoned, cigar in mouth, and his hands fumbling
at his braces, in the corridor. They will not be subject to the
insult of coming upon such a personage seated with the door
open.' What is not revealed is how or where the contents of the
metal box were disposed of after use.

No tourist travelled unless suitably attired, and Samuel Brothers
of Ludgate Hill, London, advertised Suits for Tourists and
Travellers (note the distinction) which were offered at £2 10s and
£2 19s—a little less than the fire escape.

The Victorian visitor from Britain was welcomed on the
Continent. He was wealthy, his money was stable, he was the
owner of a vast empire and a way of life that was envied. But
although he might be given the best table in the restaurant and
could afford to stay in the best rooms his patronising attitude
towards those he considered his inferiors was resented. After the
Second World War all this changed. Britain's economic difficulties
ensured that the Englishman on the Continent was the poor relation. His attitude to foreigners had to change and as it was the
youth of Britain who went in their thousands into Europe they
mixed easily with their opposite numbers from Germany, France

L

and elsewhere. Higher education enabled them to converse and adapt to the countries they visited. Those with limited education also demanded to go abroad but were reluctant to venture on their own. They wanted sun and a complete change but were unwilling to contend with language difficulties and had little stomach for unfamiliar foods. As long as the sun shone, the sea was blue, the food more or less like it was at home, the drink cheaper, the night life gayer, and they were in the company of those with whom they could communicate without too much difficulty, all was well.

This had been achieved at astonishingly keen prices, but the popular resorts abroad drew thousands not only from Britain but from other countries in Europe. Such resorts are becoming as crowded as those in Britain, so the holidaymaker seeks places further afield in Africa and on remote islands, just as the Victorians fled to the Continent when the favourite seaside resorts in England were invaded by 'trippers'.

The exploitation of the holidaymaker on a package tour is familiar. Chivvied from airport lounge to plane and back again to the lounge, he does eventually arrive in the country he planned to visit (but not always). The hotel into which he has been booked may be a mere frame or, if built, over-booked. Due to currency fluctuations he was, up to 1975, surcharged on arrival or at departure (or both). He paid out the money he had hoped would be spent on the cheap drink and night life he was led to believe existed. One sees on television and in the press photographs of these unfortunates flopping down exhausted in airport lounges clutching their baggage, money and passports, victims perhaps of industrial action or, more likely, the tribulations of the travel industry balanced on a fine knife-edge between profit and loss.

But for all the troubles one hears about, there are many thousands whose package tours abroad run smoothly and who encounter no hindrances or hold-ups. The hotel—when compared with the colourful brochure pored over in the winter months—is exactly as portrayed, and a thoroughly enjoyable and worthwhile time is spent. There is even money left over for a second holiday in the spring or autumn.

As the jets roar overhead carrying those in search of a holiday there is little occasion on earth for the day outing and excursion described in this book. Life offers few surprises and it was surprise and pleasurable anticipation that were inherent in the enjoyment of the old type of outing. The rush and bustle of most forms of modern transport, the impersonality of motorways, the desecration of much of the countryside all obliterate visual enjoyment. A place that could, in the old days, be visited annually with pleasure because it was always the same can to-day be changed almost beyond recognition in the intervening twelve months. The day outing was a need; now its need is limited. People lead fuller lives, have their own means of transport into which they crowd their family and friends, odds and ends, bits and pieces and set off where the inclination takes them.

' "Nearly there!" the Queen repeated. "Why, we passed it ten minutes ago! Faster!" '

Sources

Appleby, John B. and others, *The People's Carriage 1874–1974*. Bristol Omnibus Co. Ltd, 1974

Becker, Bernard H., *Holiday Haunts*. Remington, 1884

Berlyn, Peter, *A Popular Narrative of the Origin, History, Progress and Prospects of the Great Industrial Exhibition 1851*. James Gilbert, 1851

Brooke, David, 'The Opposition to Sunday Rail Services in North East England 1834–1914'. *Journal of Transport History*, Vol. 6, No. 2. November, 1963

Burtt, Frank, *Cross-Channel and Coastal Paddle Steamers*. Tilling, 1934

Cook, Thomas, *Cook's Scottish Tourist Official Directory*. London, 1861

Cook, Thomas (compiler), *Handbook of the Trip to Liverpool*. Leicester, 1845

Corley, T. A. B., *Quaker Enterprise in Biscuits: Huntley & Palmers of Reading 1822–1872*. Hutchinson, 1972

Croft, R. J., *Transport History*, Vol. 4, No. 3, November, 1971. David & Charles

Dickens, Charles, *Sketches By Boz*

Dowding, Walter, *Thirty Years of Progress in Passenger Transport: A History of the Red and White Group of Omnibus Companies 1914–1949*

Evans, John, *An Excursion to Brighton* etc. Whittingham, 1821

Farr, A. D., *The Royal Deeside Line*. David & Charles, 1968

Fay, C. R., *Palace of Industry 1851*. C.U.P., 1951

First Report of the Commissioners for the Exhibition of 1851 to the Rt. Hon. Spencer Horatio Walpole etc. H.M.S.O., 1852

Freeling, Arthur, *Picturesque Excursions*. London, 1839

Hughes, M. Vivian, *A London Family 1870–1900*. O.U.P. 1946

Jones, Henry Festing (editor), *The Notebooks of Samuel Butler*. Fifield, 1912

Knight's Excursion Companion: Excursions from London. Charles Knight, 1851

Lardner, Dr and others, *The Great Exhibition and London in 1851*. London, 1852

Lawrence, G. C. (editor), *The British Empire Exhibition 1924. Official Guide*. Fleetway Press, 1924

Lee, Laurie, *Cider With Rosie*. The Hogarth Press, 1959

Lindsey, W. H., *A Season at Harwich with Excursions by Land and Water*. London, 1851

MacDonald, Hugh, *Days at the Coast*. Glasgow, 1857

Mate, C. H. and Riddle, C., *Bournemouth 1810–1910*. W. Mate, 1910

Maugham, W. S., *Liza of Lambeth*. Heinemann, 1966 edition

Nowell-Smith, Simon (editor), *Edwardian England 1901–1914*. O.U.P., 1964

Mayhew, Henry and Cruikshank, George, *1851: or The Adventures of Mr and Mrs Sandboys and Family who came up to London . . . to see the Great Exhibition*. London, 1851

Milner, C. (editor), *Odds and Ends: A Manuscript Magazine*, Vol. XV. St Paul's Mutual Improvement Society, Manchester, 1869

Mitchell, Charles, *The Long Watch*. The Sailor's Children's Society, 1961

Nodal, John H. (editor), *Manchester Notes and Queries*, Vol. VIII. Manchester & London, 1891

Ottley, George, *A Bibliography of British Railway History*. George Allen & Unwin, 1966

Paterson, Alan J. S., *The Victorian Summer of the Clyde Steamers*. David & Charles, 1972

Patterson, Edward M., *The Londonderry and Lough Swilly Railway*. David & Charles/Macdonald, 1964

Pearson, R. E., 'Railways in Relation to Resort Development in East Lincolnshire'. *East Midland Geographer*, Vol. 4, Part 5, June 1968

Plomer, William (editor), *Kilvert's Diary. Selections from the Diary of the Rev. Francis Kilvert 1 January 1870–19 August 1871 and from 23 August 1871–19 August 1872*. Cape, 1938 and 1939

Pimlott, J. A. R., *The Englishman's Holiday*. Faber, 1947

Rae, W. Fraser, *The Business of Travel*. Thos. Cook & Son, 1891

Roscoe, Thomas, *Summer Tour to the Isle of Wight*. Harwood, 1843

Sitwell, Osbert, *The Scarlet Tree*. Macmillan, 1956

Stretton, Clement E., *The History of the Midland Railway*. Methuen, 1901

Summerly, Felix, *Day's Excursions*. London, 1843

Summerly, Felix, *Pleasure Excursions*. London, 1846

Sunday Excursions. Household Tracts for the People. Jarrold, 1863

Sunday on 'The Line' or Plain Facts for the Working Men. London, 1863

Swinglehurst, Edmund, *The Romantic Journey: the Story of Thomas Cook and Victorian Travel*. Pica Editions, 1974

Thomas, John, 'The Regional Histories of the Railways of Great Britain', Vol. VI, *Scotland: The Lowlands and Borders*. David and Charles, 1971

Thomas, John, *The West Highland Railway*. David & Charles, 1965

Tressel, Robert, *The Ragged Trousered Philanthropists*. Panther edition, 1967

Williams, Frederick S., *Our Iron Roads: their History, Construction and Social Influences*. Ingram, Cooke, 1852

In addition to the journals mentioned in the text:

Great Western Railway Magazine, The London & North Eastern Railway Magazine, The P.L.A. Monthly, Railway Chronicle, The Railway Gazette, Railway & Travel Monthly, South Western Gazette, Transport & Travel Monthly

The following companies, organisations and societies supplied material from their archives and records:

B.P. Trading Ltd
Dr Barnardo's
Bentalls
Blackie & Son Ltd
The Boots Co. Ltd
Chubb & Son's Lock & Safe Co. Ltd
Clarke, Nicholls & Coombs Ltd
Thomas Cook & Son Ltd
Thomas Coram Foundation for Children
George Ewer & Co. Ltd
Faire Bros & Co. Ltd
Ferranti Ltd
Kodak Ltd
Laurence, Scott & Electromotors Ltd
Charles Letts & Co. Ltd
The John Lewis Partnership

National Bus Company and companies within the group
National Children's Homes
The North Eastern Children's Society
The Omnibus Society
Pilkington Brothers Ltd
Reckitt & Colman Products Ltd
Rowntree Mackintosh Ltd
J. Sainsbury Ltd
The Sailors' Children's Society
The Shaftesbury Society
W. H. Smith & Son Ltd
Times Newspapers Ltd
Unilever Ltd
Church Education and R.E. Resources Centre, Westhill, Birmingham
Wiggins Teape Ltd

The following County Record Offices and Libraries supplied material from their archives and records:

County of Bedford Record Office
Reference Library, Birmingham Public Libraries
Archives Office, Buckinghamshire County Council
East Sussex County Record Office
Essex Record Office
Humberside County Record Office
Archives Office, Kent County Council
Archives Department, Manchester Public Libraries
Central Library, Newcastle-upon-Tyne

Norfolk Record Office
Nottinghamshire Record Office
Northumberland County Record Office
District Central Library, Preston
Public Record Office
Salop County Record Office
Central Library, Southend-on-Sea
Staffordshire County Record Office
Suffolk Record Office
Wakefield District Library Headquarters
Warwickshire County Record Office

Index

Note. The subject-matter of the text illustrations is included in the index
fp indicates frontispiece.

Aberdeen 29, 133
Aboyne 133
Akenfield 106
Alcohol, dangers of 82, 83, 84
Aldburgh fp
Allied Paper Merchants 147
Allport, James 107
Anti-Sunday Travelling Union 52
Ardrossen 98
Armathwaite 67
Arnold, Dr 48
Arrocher 98
Arundel 51
Ashby-de-la-Zouch 63
Ashington 137
Astor, Lady Violet 135
Astor, Major 134
Atkins Bros. & Co. 68
Ayr 98

Balgarnie, Rev. R. 84
Banchory 29
Bands, *see* Music
Bank Holiday Act (1871), the 25
Barnardo's, Dr 82–4, 86, 87
Barnes (cotton spinner), Mr 59
Bass, Ratcliffe & Gretton 128
Battle Bridge Congregational Chapel
    107, 108
Bedford 109
Bell, Mr George, recollections 115,
    116
Bentalls 142
Beverley 125
Binnie, Rev. A. 94
Birkenhead 59, 69
Birmingham 102, 107, 122, 128
Bishopstoke 49
Blackie & Son Ltd 69, 70
Blackpool 29, 146, 147, 149, 150
Blunden, Edmund 114
Bodmin 132
Bolton 59
Boots the Chemists 128, 129, 130

Bournemouth 82, 93, 144
Bowling 99
Box Hill 51
Boyes, William 148
Bremmer, Dr 29
Bridlington 116, 138, 152
Brierdean Bridge 92
Brighton 19, 23, 31, 32, 43, 51, 53, 60,
    67, 68, 153, 160
Bristol 128, 139, 140
British & Colonial Printer, The 18, 19
Broxbourne 18, 19
Buckfastleigh 115
Buncrana 132
Burnham Beeches 113
Burnley 29, 142
Burns, Rev. W. C. 50
Burr, George 94
Burton-on-Trent 128
Butler, Samuel 43, 44
Buttermere 64, 65

Caerphilly 131
Canal excursions 90, 102
Carlisle 64, 95
Carrow Abbey 60, 75
Carrow First Day Schools 72–5
Carters Association, the 99
Chance Bros. 61
Chanctonbury Ring 156
Charabancs and coaches 20, 38, 39,
    113, 114, 115, 117, 137, 139–53, 155,
    156
Charities' outings 19, 28, 77–89, 124,
    155
Cheddar 139, 144
Chingford 37, 38
Chippenham 34
Christ's Hospital 124
Cider With Rosie 113, 114
Clacton 19, 44
Clarke, Nicholls & Coombs, 136
Claughton, Miss R. F., recollections
    117, 118

Cleethorpes 46, 47, 150
Clent Hills, the 52, 107
Clevedon 139
Clyde Steamers 98–100
Clyde Wharf Sugar Refinery 45
Coatbridge Phoenix Ironworks 100
Cobham 24, 25
Cockermouth 54, 55
Colchester 142
Colman, Geoffrey 75
Colman, J. & J. Ltd 60, 73, 145
Colman, Jeremiah and Caroline 74
Colman, the Misses 72, 73, 75
Colne 29
Cook, Thomas 39–41, 44, 53, 63, 70
  73, 121, 132, 133, 137
Cookham 101
Coombe Lodge 101
Correlli, Marie 88
Crarae Quarry disaster 99, 100
Cromer 75
Croydon 24
Crystal Palace 60, 126, 131, 133
Cummersdale 64, 65, 66, 95

Darlington 102, 143
Deal 47, 48
Delgado, G. 17–21
Derby 107
Derby, Earl of 26
Derry 132
Dorking 51
Dovedale 114
Dovercourt 29
Dress 17, 24, 30, 31, 32, 38, 40, 46,
  57, 58, 59, 60, 64, 76, 78, 85, 86, 91,
  119, 123
Driffield 116
Druiridge Bay 138
Dudley 52
Du Garde Peach, Dr L. 142
Dumbarton 99
Dunlop Rubber Co. 128
Dunoon 99

Eastcote 72, 140
Ecroyd & Sons, Wm 67
Edinburgh, 25, 64, 116, 133
Elstree 19
'England, Excursion To' 25
Epping 86, 109, 136
Epsom 28, 140, 145

Eskdalemuir 115
Evening Standard 128
'Excursion Train' (song), 'The' 31–3,
  90
Excursions: to Continent 46, 157; to
  Duke of Wellington's funeral 132;
  to hangings 131, 132; to hopfields
  146; to London, *see* London; to
  shops 140, 142, 159, 160; to sporting events 28, 57, 131, 133, 137, 138,
  140, 145, 155; to stately homes 146;
  to theatres, entertainments 133, 137,
  140, 142, 143, 146; to White Star
  liners, 146
Exhibitions 39, 46, 61, 74, 121–31

Factory Act (1833), the 25
Faire Brother & Porter, 62, 64
Faire Bros & Co. 130
Fancott, Mr T. R., recollections 95
Farr, James 43
Fawbert and Barnard's School 124
Felixstowe 106
Ferranti Ltd 126
Ferranti, S. Z. de 67
Filey 38, 39
Firms' outings 17–21, 45, 58–62, 64–
  76, 126, 128, 129, 133–6, 140, 141,
  147, 148, 149, 150, 151, 157–9
Fleetwood 28, 29, 43, 59, 88
Folkestone 143
Food and drink: to 1914 fp, 17, 18,
  21, 30, 32, 33, 43, 59, 60, 65, 66, 67,
  68, 69, 70, 71, 72, 73, 74, 78, 79,
  80, 83, 85, 86, 90, 91, 92, 93, 107,
  108, 109, 110, 112, 115, 123, 126,
  127, 131, 136, 137, 149; thereafter
  103, 104, 105, 106, 113, 115, 116,
  117, 118, 120, 135, 137, 138, 141,
  145, 147, 149, 150, 151
Foster, Mr William, recollections 116
Fountain's Abbey 34, 35
Franklin, Canon 78
Free Ragged Schools 82, 87
Fresh Air Fund, the 80, 88
Fry & Son, J. S. 128, 152

Garlochhead 98
Garner, Mr E. J., recollections 137
Gateshead 132
General Steam Navigation Co. 91, 103
Glasgow 64, 69, 79, 98, 99, 100, 142

Gloucester 132
Goodyear, R. A. H. 149
Goole 96
Gore, G. 93
Gossages & Son, William 128
Gourock 99
Gravesend 93
Greenhithe 93
Greenock 99
Gretna Green 133
Guest, Keen & Nettlefolds 128
Guildford 24

Hampton Court 51, 60
Harper, Charles G. 145
Harrogate 34, 147
Hastings 19, 20, 30, 31, 47, 51, 60, 68, 114
Hastings & St Leonard's Weekly Times 68
Hawes 138
Hayley Park 52
Hever 24, 134–6
Holiday Haunts 42
Home & Colonial Stores 68
Horner, Mrs A. B., recollections 117
Horse-drawn vehicle excursions 20, 37, 38, 42, 87, 109, 110, 111, 112, 113, 114, 143, 149, 155
Hull 50, 53, 96, 138, 147
Hunstanton 118, 119, 120
Huntley & Palmers 45, 60, 75, 101, 126, 128
Huddersfield 124

Ilfracombe 97
Illustrated London News 27, 56–7, 122
Illustrated Times 30, 47
Ingleton 117
Ipswich 55, 145
Isle of Wight 94, 95, 108, 143

Kenilworth 94, 95
Kennington 23
Killin 69, 70
Kilvert, Rev. Francis 30, 33, 34, 43, 44, 96–8
Knaresborough 34
Knight, Charles 23, 26, 27
Knowsley 26
Kodak Ltd 144, 151

Langley Marish School Board 108
Largs 99
Leeds 132, 133, 142, 147
Leicester 39, 40, 57, 62, 63, 130
Leicester Chronicle 40
Leicester Guardian 58, 61
Leicester Journal 40
Lever Bros 46, 68, 128, 129, 147, 148
Littlehampton 51
Liverpool 28, 59, 81, 82, 117, 122, 132
Liverpool, Handbook of the Trip to 53
Liza of Lambeth 33, 37, 38
Lizard, the 110
Llangollen 56
Loch Fyne 99
Loch Lomond 98
Loch Long 98
Lochgoilhead 99
Lochmaben 115
London, Excursions to 27, 51, 68, 72, 73–4, 122–30, 132, 133, 137, 142
Lowestoft 75
Lyman, Mrs E. A., recollections 102, 110, 111

Maidstone 48
Manchester 28, 35, 36, 37, 115, 122, 131
Mardon, Son and Hall 128
Margate 17, 19, 75, 103, 104, 114
Mayhew, Henry and George Cruikshank 54, 55
Mazawattee Tea Co. 68
Metropolitan Vickers 128
Middlesbrough 138
Miners' excursions 53, 96, 136–8, 150
Monkseaton 78
Morecambe 116, 149, 150
Morris Motors 152
Mullion 110
Mundsley 75
Music, singing: to 1914 18, 19, 26, 37, 40, 42, 43, 47, 51, 59, 60, 62, 63, 64, 65, 67, 69, 72, 75, 79, 81, 82, 86, 90, 91, 92, 93, 94, 99, 101, 107, 114, 115, 124, 131, 136, 138; thereafter 106, 112, 117, 118, 135, 144, 148, 150, 151, 152
Mutton (caterer) 19
'Mystery' tours 141, 142, 154, 156

National Sunday League 51, 52
Nelson (Lancs) 67
Newcastle-upon-Tyne 28, 50, 77, 78, 79, 138, 143
Newcastle-upon-Tyne Poor Children's Holiday Association 78
Newton Bridge 28
Normanton 34
North East Children's Society 78
North Gawber 53, 96
Northfleet 93
Norwich 73, 145
Nottingham 39, 40, 57, 128

Offerton School 82
Orford fp
Oxford 115, 152, 153

Paignton 141
Paley (employer), Mr 59, 60
Palmer brothers, the, *see* Huntley & Palmers
Pardoe, Miss M., recollections 102
Paris and the Parisians 161
Park Place (Henley) 101
Parker, Rev. J. 48
Partick 99
Peak Frean's 45
Pearson, C. Arthur 80
Penster Hill 132
Penzance 34
Pevensey Bay 155
Picnics 63, 86, 87, 136
Picturesque Excursions 53
Pilkington Bros 149, 150
Pinner 72, 140
Plymouth 110, 143
Pontypridd 131
Poor Children's Outing Fund 89
Portsmouth 60, 75, 94, 108
Port Sunlight 46, 68, 128, 147
Preston 26, 28, 43, 55, 59, 60, 88, 148

Ragged School Union 80
Ragged Trousered Philanthropists, The 70, 71
Railway excursion train, the: accidents on 55–7; cultural benefits of 27–51; evils of 43; song about 31–3; safety of 40, 41, 52–7, 107
Railway's Gardening Competition 138

Railways (1840), a Select Committee on 25
Ramsgate 51, 75, 103
Reading 60, 101, 128
Redhill 145
Reigate 30
Renfrew 99
Rhyl 35, 36, 37
Ripon 34, 35
River excursions 90, 100, 101, 104, 105
Roberts and Archer's Dramatic Company 94
Rochester Bridge 93
Rothesay 79, 100
Royal Benefit Society 108

'Safety' Omnibus, The 29
Sailors' Children's Society 84
Sainsbury, J. B. 104
St Leonard's, 51
Samuel Brothers (outfitters) 161
Sandgate 19
Scarborough 38, 84, 111, 112, 138, 147, 148, 149
Scarlet Tree, The 38, 39
Sceneaidicator, The 145
Sheerness 93
Shepperton 24
Sheringham 75
Shoreham 53
Shrewsbury, Earl of 44
Silloth 95, 116
Skegness 46, 150
Sketches by Boz 90–3
Smith & Son, W. H. 72, 101, 144, 148, 149
Southampton 49, 50, 60, 93, 95
Southend 45, 46, 51, 103, 107, 108, 109
Southend Standard 45
Spithead 93
Sports, pastimes 18, 62, 63, 67, 68, 72, 79, 81, 86, 103, 109, 120, 135, 147, 150
Squires, Mr C., recollections 147
Stafford Photographic Society 155, 156
Stanley 89
Stead, McAlpine 64, 65, 95, 96
Steamer excursions fp, 28, 59, 78–9, 82, 90–105, 108
Stranraer 141

Stuart, Mrs, sister of the Misses Colman 72, 75
Studley Park 34, 35
Sunday School excursions 20, 102, 106–20, 115, 150, 155
Sunday School Union 107
Sunday Times 155
Sunday travel 44, 48–52, 132
Sutherland, Millicent Duchess of 81
Sutton Bridge 118, 120
Sutton Park 107
Swanage 82, 94
Sydenham, David 93, 94

Tabbutt & Co. 30
Taylor, Mr A. J., recollections 118–20
Taylor, Mrs L., recollections 109
Teignmouth 115
Temperance Excursion Committee, The 88
Temperance influence, the 29, 39, 41, 65, 70, 88, 101, 110, 124. *See also* Alcohol
Theydon Bois, 82, 83
Thomas & Brothers, Ltd, Christopher 140
Thorpe & Co. R. 96
Times, The 28, 134–6
Torquay 141
Tripconey, Mrs E., recollections 110
'Trippers', attitudes towards and behaviour of 42–6, 47, 48, 147

Troon 98
Truro 34
Turvey Village School 109
Tynemouth 78

Union Jack Shoeblack Brigade 84–6

Wadebridge 132
Walton 23, 24, 30
Walton and The Sokens 29
Weaverthorpe 111
Wednesbury 44
Wells 139, 144
Weston-super-Mare 97, 113, 139
Weybridge 23, 24, 30
Whitbread, C. C. 109
Whitby 138
Whitley Bay 89, 116
Widnes 128
Wigram, Archdeacon 49, 50
Willson, Mrs P., recollections 112, 113
Wilson, Mr H., recollections 111, 112
Wilson, Walter 79
Winchester 24, 49, 94
Windsor 101
Workington 54, 55
Wycombe Abbey 112

Yarmouth 75
York 40, 138